D0081551

Using
QUALITATIVE RESEARCH
in ADVERTISING

Using QUALITATIVE RESEARCH in ADVERTISING

Strategies, Techniques, and Applications

Margaret A. Morrison
University of Tennessee

Eric Haley
University of Tennessee

Kim Bartel Sheehan
University of Oregon

Ronald E. Taylor
University of Tennessee

SAGE Publications
International Educational and Professional Publisher
Thousand Oaks ▪ London ▪ New Delhi

For information:

Sage Publications, Inc.
2455 Teller Road
Thousand Oaks, California 91320
E-mail: order@sagepub.com

Sage Publications Ltd.
6 Bonhill Street
London EC2A 4PU
United Kingdom

Sage Publications India Pvt. Ltd.
M-32 Market
Greater Kailash I
New Delhi 110 048 India

Printed in the United States of America

Library of Congress Cataloging-in-Publication Data

Using qualitative research in advertising: Strategies, techniques, and applications / by Margaret A. Morrison . . . [et al.].
   p. cm.
Includes bibliographical references and index.
ISBN 0-7619-2599-6 — ISBN 0-7619-2383-7 (p)
   1. Advertising—Research.   2. Market research—Methodology.
3. Qualitative research.   I. Morrison, Margaret A.
HF5814 .U78   2002
659.1′07′2—dc21

                                                      2002000278

This book is printed on acid-free paper.

02 03 04 05 10 9 8 7 6 5 4 3 2 1

Acquisitions Editor:	Marquita Flemming
Editorial Assistant:	MaryAnn Vail
Copy Editor:	Kris Bergstad
Production Editor:	Diane S. Foster
Typesetter:	Graphicraft Limited
Proofreader:	Toni Williams
Indexer:	Molly Hall
Cover Designer:	Michelle Lee

Contents

Acknowledgments

W e would like to acknowledge the following people for their help with or support of this book: Andre Chinn, Charles Frazer, Ann Maxwell, Erik Bledsoe, Joyce Holloway, Mariea Hoy, Roxanne Hovland, Michael Hoefges, Sally McMillan, Lynne Taggart of the APGUS, Brenda Campbell, Kate Gregory, Heath Overton, Jenessa Powell, Valerie Salinas, Stephanie Sheridan, Thomas Williams, and the account planners across the United States who were willing to talk with us and respond to our surveys.

1

Introduction and Overview

Advertising, as you've probably noticed, surrounds every facet of your life. Indeed, industry estimates suggest that more than $480 billion will be spent on advertising in 2001, with over half of that in the United States alone (Coen, 2001). That translates into millions of ads, all vying for the attention of consumers. In some instances, advertisers are looking for the attention of very specific, targeted groups of consumers (e.g., adults aged 25–54 who are liberal, recycle regularly, entertain at least twice a month, and have minimum household incomes of $75,000). In other instances, targeted audiences may be more general (e.g., working moms). Regardless of the target, marketers have become very savvy in using research to create messages that are relevant, timely, and motivating to the audience they want to reach.

This is a book about how to use a particular type of research—qualitative research—to inspire great advertising. Qualitative research refers to "the meanings, concepts, definitions, characteristics, metaphors, symbols, and descriptions of things" (Berg, 1989, p. 2). It is an approach to research that uses a variety of methods and involves an interpretive, naturalistic approach to whatever is the focus of study (Denzin & Lincoln, 1994). Its greatest utility is in discovering underlying meanings and patterns in relationships. The character of qualitative research makes it and its associated methods extremely useful for uncovering complex consumer insights that can lead to successful advertising.

In writing this book, we've tried to adopt a consumer perspective. That is, we're convinced that great advertising comes only from an understanding of consumers' want and needs. And, in order to understand those wants and needs, the consumer needs to be consulted and integrated at virtually every step of the research process. In short, the strategies and techniques outlined in this book are

1

based on something called an account planning philosophy. We'll talk about this philosophy in just a moment.

We wrote this book for several different audiences. Primarily, account planners will find this book a valuable resource, particularly given the few formal training programs that are around today. In a national U.S. survey of account planners that we conducted, only 45% of respondents reported that they had received formal on-the-job training (55% didn't receive any formal training), and 95% reported receiving only informal on-the-job training. Less than half of respondents reported receiving training in qualitative research methods. Qualitative methods was one of the most cited areas by planners when we asked them, "In what areas do you feel you need more training?" Yet our survey also uncovered that qualitative methods are commonly used by account planners. Given that account planners are often involved in qualitative research but receive little training in how to use qualitative methods, we saw the need for a book that planners can turn to as they go about the difficult task of trying to develop consumer insights.

Of course, account planners aren't the only ones who might find value in this book. Others who might find this book helpful include research suppliers who, given their relationship with account planners, want to understand the role of qualitative research a bit better; advertising agencies, who will find it a useful addition to the reference libraries; and training programs and universities offering classes in advertising.

A Brief History of Account Planning

In order to put our later discussions of particular types of research into context, a brief overview of the history and nature of account planning is in order. Account planning was developed in the mid-1960s and can be traced to the U.K. offices of two advertising agencies—J. Walter Thompson and Boase Massimi Pollitt (now BMP DDB; Steel, 1998). Account planning originated from a need to better understand the increasingly complex consumer landscape, synergize research, and bring a consumer focus into the process of message generation.

By the 1960s, society was undergoing great changes and that meant that the nature of consumerism was also changing. Think about it. Before World War II, women stayed home and cared for their kids, and men headed off to earn the household paycheck. That all changed with World War II. More and more women entered the workplace, and the dynamics of the household—especially with regard to product purchasing—changed dramatically. Instead of cooking meals from scratch and keeping a spotless home, modern working women looked for foods that required little preparation and products that helped to cut down on the time it took to clean house. As a result, whole new product categories emerged that catered to the needs of modern women. Then, the women's liberation movement changed the landscape even more. Suddenly, advertisers weren't sure how to speak to these modern women.

That's just one example; we don't want to give you the idea that account planning grew solely out of the women's liberation movement. Other cultural changes, such as the leveling of racial attitudes, the growth of technology, the emergence of the credit industry, and the rise of health and fitness concerns, were also occurring. The fact is that the entire social landscape was changing and the influence on advertising and consumer purchasing habits was dramatic. That's even truer today, and evidence abounds that consumers don't adopt just one lifestyle or consume products according to a single set of attitudes (Piirto, 1990).

The business landscape of the 1960s was also changing. Consumer research was being somewhat diluted across the marketing, advertising, and media research departments of both advertising agencies and clients. The number of independent companies conducting market research—research suppliers—escalated. These companies specialized in generating and selling information about consumers. One of the biggest purchasers of this information was advertising agencies. As a result, advertising agencies found themselves deluged with information, both from their internal research departments as well as from new, external agencies. Although this information was useful to ad agencies for learning more about consumers, the surge in available research resulted in agencies being so inundated with data that the account management team—which was in charge of coordinating the agency's efforts—was often not using it in the most efficient manner.

It wasn't only the account team that was having trouble processing and using all that research. Lisa Fortini-Campbell (2001) notes that members of creative departments grew resistant to research that they saw as impeding their art. In part, this resistance stemmed from the way research was being used, not that there was so much of it. Research was being used to copytest advertisements as opposed to being used to develop advertising. So, research was being used to correct or shoot down ads that creatives had already invested a substantial amount of time in instead of being used in a diagnostic manner. And, when research was used in the early stages of advertising development, it often went no farther than the token focus group. Creatives often viewed the research imposed on them—whether from internal or external research factions—as lacking a basic understanding of the consumer and the problem at hand. The deluge of research information, coupled with the misuse of research in the creative process, meant that agencies were continuing to produce advertising without fully understanding what drove these new, complex consumers.

Account planning, then, grew out of the changing consumer environment and the advertising agency's need for a single department to assemble and analyze relevant product data holistically and apply it to the day-to-day decision making on an account. In addition, account planning's popularity is also attributable to the fact that the presence of an account planning department positions agencies as having exceptional creative solutions and sets them apart from competitors during the all-important stage of pitching new business (Barry, Peterson, & Todd, 1987; Maxwell, Wanta, & Bentley, 2000). Agencies with account planning departments essentially integrate functions formerly conducted by other departments in the agency or by outside market research consultants, and seek to add a consumer perspective to all aspects of advertising development. This integration allows agencies to position themselves as strategic partners with their clients and to retain control over business that might otherwise be contracted out to independent research companies.

And so account planning developed, gained in popularity, and spread to the rest of Europe during the 1970s. In 1982, account planning was "discovered" by Jay Chiat of Chiat/Day and introduced to the United States, where it was widely embraced (Steel, 1998). According to the Account Planning Group U.S. (the APG:US is the largest professional association of account planners), by 1995, over 250 people were employed in account planning in the Unites States, a figure that grew to more than 1,000 in 1999. Account planning departments are now fairly common in the U.S. advertising industry and are found in large full-service agencies as well as medium-sized agencies and smaller creative boutiques (Nelson & Kent, 1999). Attendance at the annual APG:US conference increased from less than 50 to more than 950 between 1994 and 2000. At the 2000 conference, organizers commented that planning has grown beyond just bringing the consumer's voice to the table. Now, planning is used to understand all aspects of a client's business such as corporate culture, management's values, the meaning of products to the workers who make them, and other important information that can inform message strategy development.

The Function of Planning

What exactly do account planners do? Account planners function as liaisons between the account executive and the creative department, and between the creative department and the consumer. In theory, account planners are fully integrated members of the account and creative teams. In practice, the structure of planning across agencies varies somewhat: In some agencies the planning function leans more toward account management, and at others planners are considered members of creative departments (Kover & Goldberg, 1995). Nevertheless, it is generally agreed that a planner is a point person in the process of developing message strategy, the "primary contact with the outside world; the person who, through personal background, knowledge of all pertinent information, and overall experience, is able to bring a strong consumer focus to all advertising decisions" (White, 1995, p. 18).

The primary responsibility of planners is to understand the target audience and then represent it throughout the entire advertising development process. In fact, account planners work so closely with the target audiences they study that they are often referred to as "consumer advocates" (Kover, James, & Sonner, 1997). It is this intensive interaction with consumers and creative strategy development that distinguishes account planners from more traditional market researchers (Barry et al., 1987; Capon & Scammon, 1979). In fact, account planners are also known as creative researchers or strategic researchers.

Account planners attempt to understand and represent the target audience through the use of market and research data in areas such as the product, the category, the market, the competition, and the client. The understanding that flows from the research that account planners do leads to usable insights that can help creative and account management teams produce advertising that's relevant to the target market. Effective consumer insights elicit reactions that motivate consumers to try and continue buying a product.

The Role of Research
in the Day-to-Day Activities of Account Planners

Account planners use a variety of research techniques to develop consumer insights, and they rely heavily on qualitative research, which provides the opportunity for intimate consumer contact and a less structured environment that allows for insight into the more emotional aspects of a brand. These techniques include traditional approaches such as one-on-one interviewing and focus groups, as well as more innovative approaches like accompanied shopping, word associations, use of visual prompts, video montages, projective techniques, and consumer diaries. The use of experts (such as semioticians, ethnographers, and cultural anthropologists) is also common; although these people might not work in market research, they often offer unique insights into a particular consumer situation. Account planners also track data on social and cultural changes from long-term studies that may be linked to advertising success. While doing their jobs, they conduct primary research and utilize secondary research sources such as published market reports, usage and attitude surveys, and awareness tracking studies.

The variety of research techniques used by account planners suggests two things. First, no single research technique can do everything; it's important to recognize the advantages and disadvantages of each method. All sources of information are valuable, but they are also flawed because they are limited in scope and may not contain the total answer to a given problem. Knowledge of the various research approaches is necessary to understand the scope of a consumer's personal experience and neutralize biases ("Healthy Research," 1982). Although we know that planners rely primarily on interviews and focus groups, smart planners know that these approaches won't always yield the information they are trying to uncover. In fact, at the 1999 APG:US conference several of the topics discussed dealt with the overuse of focus groups, the gist of the idea being that planners were using these groups without really considering whether they were the best way to tap into consumer insights.

Second, planners must be familiar with alternative research methods so they can intelligently evaluate the array of research options available to them. It is important to remember that qualitative research is not synonymous with just focus groups. Innovation, in the life of a planner, means finding the best and most appropriate way of talking to consumers, one that will yield the information that will lead to a great creative strategy. Often, that means much more than conducting focus groups or interviews. The number of new research techniques on the market is startling, and planners must be able to make cogent choices among varying options as they go about the important business of uncovering consumer insights. We hope this book will help you make these choices.

Although many of the techniques used by account planners are similar to those used by other research functions in an agency, account planning differs from more traditional research in that the research incorporated becomes part of the process instead of being used in an advisory or evaluative capacity. In this way, consumers become part of the advertising process because the account planner gives them a voice (hence the label consumer advocate). For example, though more traditional research can produce consumer insights, an account planner takes these consumer insights, interprets them, and advises the creative team how they can be used to develop creative strategy. In essence, the research used by account planners is more focused and integral to problem solving than is the case with traditional research, and the ability of planners to contribute intelligent insights to their findings determines whether they are full partners in the creative process. Planners often find that they are aided in their interpretations of data by input from account managers, creatives, clients, or agency management.

Although this book focuses on using qualitative research in an innovative manner to develop creative strategies, you need to know that innovation doesn't end with simply being research savvy. Innovation also means being alert and aware of your research surroundings so that you can make connections between seemingly unconnected things. These are the types of connections that help you uncover the consumer insights that lead to great advertising.

Stages of Account Planning

Account planning is aimed at generating consumer insights during two key phases of the campaign process: brand/creative strategy development and evaluation of campaign effectiveness. Lisa Fortini-Campbell (2001), in her book about generating consumer insights, *Hitting the Sweet Spot*, further divides the brand/creative strategy development stage into the following stages: (a) discovering/defining the advertising task; (b) preparing the creative brief; (c) developing the creative; and (d) presenting the advertising to the client. The techniques discussed in other chapters of this book have differing degrees of utility depending on the stage of account planning. In advance of these chapters, it is important to differentiate what happens at each stage.

Brand/strategy development is the main aspect of a planner's job because it lays the groundwork for creative executions that effectively communicate to consumers in a way that is relevant and meaningful. Fortini-Campbell notes that a planner must first gather and assimilate information about consumers and their environment from every source available. She mentions the importance of reviewing such things as secondary research and sales data and of conducting primary research to find out everything possible about the environment the product inhabits. Pam Scott, a leader in the field of account planning, notes that the target market's relationship with the product, the brand, the product category, and any cultural influences must all be considered prior to determining creative strategy (Scott, 1999). Research at this point is imperative in order to discover what communication needs to occur with consumers: one must know the problem before one can diagnose and treat it.

After research has been conducted, a planner must assemble and organize it in such a way that consumer insights are highlighted and extraneous information not important to creative strategy is culled. To streamline this process, the planner prepares a creative brief. The purpose of the brief is to help guide the creative team as it conceptualizes advertising strategy designed to meet the objectives of the campaign. Scott (1999) notes that possible components of a creative brief focus on answers to the following questions: Why is the product being advertised? What is the advertising supposed to do? Who is the target market? What is known about the target market that will help with the advertising? What is the main thought that needs to be expressed? and, What are possible ways to communicate the main thought in the advertising?

It is also important to note that the creative brief is more than just the answers to these questions. According to Steel (1998), a brief is an ad to influence the creative team. Along this line, Scott (1999) notes that the brief should tell a story about the product's target audience, but that a planner must keep in mind that the real target audience for the creative brief is the people who will read and use it, namely the creative team. She recommends the use of humor, stories, and anecdotes delivered in an innovative manner designed to inspire the creative team.

Once the brief has been delivered to the creative team, rough versions of the advertisements can be prepared. But the planner's job does not end with simply delivering the brief. As advertisements are developed, the planner's function at this stage is to verify the ads with the target market. All good advertising and communications campaigns begin with clearly set objectives; to be considered successful, the campaign must meet these objectives. While consumers are fickle and no advertising is a sure bet, practitioners and clients want as much of a guarantee as is possible to ensure that the message strategy of a campaign is on target. Hence the planner tests rough versions of ads against the target market. In evaluating the creative with the target, a planner might conduct group or one-on-one interviews with consumers in order to check that the advertisements are actually articulating the message strategy and are on track to reach the goals of the campaign. During these interviews, rough or "comp" versions of the ads are shown to participants, followed by intensive questioning on the part of the planner. It's worth noting that although this discussion of evaluation has focused on evaluating the creative in rough or comp forms, planners also evaluate the consumer's response to the campaign during and after its run. According to Douglas Atkin (1997), a noted figure in the field of account planning, "planners' ultimate responsibility is accountability for effectiveness" (p. 34).

Account planners are also often involved in presenting advertisements to potential or existing clients. Fortini-Campbell notes that at this stage the planner represents the consumer's point of view and helps explain how the advertisements under consideration are in line with the campaign strategy. Planners also offer insights to the client concerning how the campaign will perform with the target audience once it has been executed. It's worth mentioning here that the presence of an account planner at a business pitch for a new account often results in an agency winning the account.

Examples

To get an idea of the importance of conducting research prior to developing brand/creative strategy, one only needs to look at some case histories of clients that have benefited from the insights uncovered by planning. Once every 2 years the APG:US gives out awards for what it considers to be exemplary examples of planning practice (APG:US, 2001). These awards are given on the basis of insight, creativity, and effectiveness. In selecting finalists for the awards, judges consider the business background of the product for which the campaign was designed, the communication objectives of the campaign, descriptions of brand and consumer insights that have been developed, and explanations of the creative strategy and guidelines for campaign evaluation. Several high-profile campaigns have earned the attention of the APG:US based on the contribution of account planning to the final marketing solution.

http://www.moneygram.com

MONEYGRAM

If you've ever sent someone money electronically, you know that your options are limited to a couple of companies that do business in this category. The best known of these is Western Union, which in the 1990s enjoyed an 80% market share and outspent its major competitor, MoneyGram, three to one on advertising. Western Union also had twice as many locations as MoneyGram, and an incredible 99% awareness level among consumers (compared with MoneyGram's 60% awareness; "Campbell Mithun Esty: MoneyGram," 1999).

Even though MoneyGram's sales had been declining for more than 2 years, it did have one advantage over Western Union: MoneyGram's service was 5 dollars cheaper than comparable service from Western Union. And, MoneyGram's price included a free phone card and 10-word message to the recipient of the money transfer. However, while price was important to the target audience for the brand, on the surface it didn't lend itself well to forming the basis of the brand's image.

The advertising agency Campbell Mithun Esty (CME) faced the challenge of transforming MoneyGram's price advantage from a product feature into a brand image. Planners from the agency went to urban neighborhoods to talk to MoneyGram's primary target market: African American women. Taking an ethnographic approach, they sought to understand these women's lives and to gain insight into their experiences with electronic money transfers and their feelings about Western Union and MoneyGram.

Several key findings emerged from their research. First, these women felt taken advantage of. This was true of their general feeling toward life as well as their wire transfer experiences. These women took care of those around them, but they sometimes couldn't help but feel a bit resentful about it. In helping out their family and friends by wiring money, they were, in essence, giving away their hard-earned cash. And, they had to pay a fee to do so! So it's no wonder that the women saw themselves as "givers" and wire transfers as "takers." This was particularly the view they held of Western Union, the category dominator. The same sentiments were voiced over and over by the target market.

It was the insight that the target market felt taken advantage of that formed the basis for the subsequent advertising that CME developed. The basis of the strategy was to make MoneyGram's cost advantage synonymous with giving back to these women. This was a strategy that worked on both rational (i.e., the cost savings) and emotional (i.e., giving as opposed to taking) levels. The executions featured a grandmotherly character who gave advice and looked out for the women in the target. This approach was supplemented with a program in which donations were made to a group that the target market was very familiar with: the Boys & Girls Clubs of America. Both qualitative and quantitative measures were used to track the success of the campaign, which resulted in a sales growth for MoneyGram after only 2 months.

YOO-HOO CHOCOLATE

Yoo-hoo chocolate drink had long been suffering from declining sales when it hired the Mad Dogs & Englishmen agency. Quantitative research had already indicated that the brand was seen as old-fashioned, boring, and "not for me." Yoo-hoo is considered part of the soft drink and beverage category, and other drinks in the category (such as Sprite or Minute Maid Juice) were seen as more hip to drink. Moreover, in interviews with mothers (the obvious target market because they generally buy soft drinks for their children) it was found that they would buy the drink for their younger children, but not their teenage children. Teenagers, especially boys, believed that Yoo-hoo was an old-fashioned drink for their little brothers and sisters, not something "adult." Because teenagers consume more soft drinks than any other group this was a major hurdle, and one

official website
http://www.drinkyoo-hoo.com

unofficial site
http://hubcap.clemson.edu

that needed to be overcome to get the brand back on track. Hence, Mad Dogs & Englishmen's initial recommendation was that Yoo-hoo target teenagers, not their moms ("Mad Dogs & Englishmen: Yoo-hoo Chocolate Drink," 1999).

Mad Dogs & Englishmen's account planning team turned to the Internet for some preliminary research and found that some teenage boys had created Web pages glorifying Yoo-hoo. The content of these pages paid homage to Yoo-hoo through such things as testimonials and photo collages. The pages revealed that for these teens, Yoo-hoo represented goodness and the ability to make things right; a calming presence that was in contrast to the edgier advertising messages of more popular soft drinks. Though this Web group was small and not representative of how most teens viewed Yoo-hoo, it did give the account planning team an idea of how to position the brand against larger competitors. The insight resulted in the facetious but charming strategy that, "Unlike other drinks, Yoo-hoo makes a bad situation better." The sheer irony of the strategy and the joke behind it was a compelling message for teens. The campaign executions showed teens in everyday situations where the purchase of Yoo-hoo made things better while its absence made things worse. All included the tagline, "Yoo-hoo chocolate drink. Buy any other beverage and you could be making a terrible mistake." As a result of the advertising, the brand's sales decline reversed and its distribution strengthened. Campaign evaluations concluded that the ads were functioning just as the strategy intended.

These are two examples of how research done by account planners was used to develop creative strategy leading to successful advertising campaigns. A look at *Adweek's* bi-annual review of APG:US award finalists reveals other notable campaigns in which account planning played a key role. These include Volkswagen's "Drivers Wanted" campaign, for which planners used one-on-one interviews and focus groups to develop the brand essence of the automobile manufacturer; Norwegian Cruise Line's "It's Different Out Here" campaign where planners concept tested its main idea through the use of an idea video; and Florida's Anti-Tobacco campaign (which later was rolled out nationally), for which members of the agency team conducted ethnographic and observational research to develop the award-winning "Truth" campaign.

Account Planning as Part
of the Overall Marketing Effort

Although the emphasis in this book is how to use qualitative research to create great advertising, it's important to note that advertising does not exist in a vacuum in today's complex marketing environment. Instead, it plays one role in an often bewildering combination of advertising, sales promotion, public relations, and personal selling. In other words, advertising functions as part of the promotion P that your marketing teacher always talked about when she was discussing the four Ps of marketing (product, price, place, and promotion). To explain this complex promotional recipe, marketers and academics coined the phrase "integrated marketing communications," or IMC. Essentially, the idea behind IMC is that a company speaks to its various publics with a singular voice, one that's closely tied to a brand's identity. In practice, this means that all forms of communication are conveying the same message. This consistent message leads to a brand personality and helps grow the equity, or value, of a brand.

The concept of IMC suggests that the strategies and techniques used in account planning can be used to inform other parts of marketing's four Ps. Account planning is primarily focused on improving the creative product, but insights generated from planning research can also improve or inform other areas of business strategy. Indeed, the theme of a recent Account Planning Group conference in Miami Beach (summer 2000) emphasized the need for planning to be integrated into all aspects of the marketing mix: product, price, place, and promotion. And it makes sense: You wouldn't want your advertising centered around building long-term equity in a brand while your sales promotion efforts are telling consumers that there's always a coupon available in the Sunday newspaper for 50 cents off the brand. These two things are at odds with each other; while your advertising may be building brand equity, your sales promotion is diluting your brand equity by telling the consumer that your product is always for sale and not worth its full price. Don't get us wrong, we've got nothing against sales promotions, we just want you to really think about what these things say to consumers and the impact that they have.

Unfortunately, it appears that account planning is not as integrated into the marketing process as it might be. A national U.S. survey of account planners that we conducted suggests that although more than 80% of account planners are "very involved" in brand strategy and creative strategy development, less than 6% indicated a high level of involvement in any of the following areas: media strategy development, public relations strategy development, or sales promotion strategy development. We hope that as you read this book, you'll see some areas where the strategies and techniques we describe can be applied to communications campaigns that go beyond traditional advertising.

Organization of This Book

This chapter serves as an introduction to this book and lays the foundation for explaining the perspective from which we're writing. Below, we briefly discuss what's in store for you in the remaining chapters.

In Chapter 2 we give you an overview of the theory behind qualitative research. We're operating here on the premise that you must understand the underpinnings of qualitative research before you can use it successfully. After all, there are many different research approaches and it's important for you to decide which approach is the best for getting at what you want to know. Quantitative methods, such as phone surveys, are often used quite successfully in advertising, as are things like one-on-one interviews or accompanied shopping. The key to using any research method correctly is knowing its appropriateness for a given situation. We hope that our theoretical discussion of qualitative research will help give you an idea of when certain techniques are or are not appropriate.

Chapter 3 deals with ethnographies and other extended contact methods. We've written this chapter with the following in mind: The best way to get to know a market is to live with that market. Ethnographic and other extended contact qualitative methods allow researchers to come as close as possible to living with a consumer group by researching that group in its natural setting. However, these methods often require a large time investment. This chapter explores these methods and presents examples of how to conduct such extended contact research projects as efficiently as possible. Examples illustrating how ethnographic methods have been successfully applied to account planning are incorporated to make the techniques more relevant to planners. The methods explored include ethnography, accompanied shopping, and panel studies with consumers, along with some case studies that illustrate how these techniques have been successfully used in the past.

Our research with account planners suggests that interviewing is their most often used and most valued technique. That's why we spend a lot of time in this book talking about interviewing techniques and how to get the most out of an interview. In Chapter 4 we discuss interviewing and its utility for account planning in great detail.

Account planners have been characterized as creative researchers. They have earned this label because their contribution helps generate advertising that is creative and resonates with the intended market. The label creative researcher also comes from the innovative research techniques used by planners to uncover consumer insights. In Chapter 5 we examine projective techniques that may be used by planners to help generate insights into consumer behavior. We give you an overview of the history of projective techniques along with their evolution as tools for market research. Descriptions of some of these techniques, as well as examples of how they can be used by account planners, are provided. These techniques include associations, completions, constructions, and expressions. Specific examples, such as the use of role playing, sentence completion, collage, and other visual prompts (e.g., bubble mapping or games like The House Where the Brand Lives) are also provided.

The Internet can be a powerful tool for uncovering consumer insights. Chapter 6 examines how account planners can use the resources and power of the Internet to conduct qualitative advertising research. The chapter begins with a short overview of the history of the Internet as a communications tool and provides an overview of ways that the Internet has been used to collect both quantitative and qualitative information. The main focus of the chapter is on describing how the Internet can be used to conduct interviews and online focus groups. We describe the benefits and limitations of both of these methods and also offer tips on how to encourage participation and candidness. Examples are included to illustrate the value of online interviewing for planners. We've also included a discussion of the ethical considerations of doing online qualitative research, including assessments of participant risk, the appropriateness of topics, and obtaining informed consent.

You've done all the research and uncovered some remarkable things. Now, the question is, how do you present the material in a way that will inspire the creative team? Chapter 7 covers two very important tasks in the job of an account planner: writing the creative brief and making research come to life. First, we discuss how account planners can create the most effective written briefs possible. An overriding theme of this section is the use of the creative brief to open creative doors, not close them. The importance of the creative brief is discussed, and we give you an overview of the different types of formats used for developing written briefs. We also address how to fine-tune the brief based on your personal knowledge and your relationship with the creative team. Topics addressed include interpreting the research results in the brief; partnering with creatives to develop briefs; writing a brief that connects with the creatives; maintaining focus in the brief; finding trigger words; and allowing for flexibility.

Inside the Qualitative World

Within the academic and professional research worlds there are a number of research traditions, all of which fall under the broad umbrella term *qualitative research*. You may encounter such terms as *ecological psychology, holistic ethnography, critical ethnography, cognitive anthropology, phenomenology, ethnomethodology, symbolic interactionism, critical inquiry, feminist scholarship,* and *case study*. What separates these traditions can be determined by examining the research tradition from which each comes and the relative amount of attention given to (a) context and environment, (b) social and cultural structures, (c) social interaction, (d) individual interpretation, and (e) individual free will. For example, critical inquiry and feminist scholarship assume that meaning and behavior are greatly influenced by existing social structures and they therefore focus on such things as how perceived gender differences, distribution of wealth and power, and cultural beliefs constrain meaning and define behavior. Ecological psychology assumes that individual environment and context are keys to understanding behavior, and symbolic interactionism assumes that patterns of social interaction are most important. Although these differences do exist, the similarities are much greater and are what bind together these different research traditions.

In qualitative research everyone is allowed to be a theorist; it would not be uncommon to find that in some situations context and structure are powerful determinants of behavior and in other situations to find that individual will and volition are more important. The flexibility of qualitative research is its greatest asset; qualitative researchers feel free to pick and choose from various research traditions and research techniques, depending on the research question and the research setting. Researchers steeped in quantitative methods, where there is often a step-by-step recipe for conducting research and where researchers have been instructed not to exercise their own judgment or insight, are ill at ease in the qualitative world. For additional discussion on the ways quantitative and qualitative researchers tend to see the world, see Taylor (1994).

Assumptions That Bind

Despite their differences of emphasis, there are certain assumptions about the nature of human behavior that almost all qualitative researchers agree on. These include seeing people as active, interpreting individuals who construct worlds of meanings and who act upon the world rather than allowing the world to act upon them.

ACTIVE INDIVIDUALS

Qualitative researchers see the world as made up of active, interpreting individuals forging purposeful lines of action to accomplish everyday life. Individuals take note of the things around them, process or assign meaning to those things, and then plan courses of action. Because meaning arises from within, behavior cannot be understood by seeking external forces and causes. Human beings are not simple responders to stimuli. Rather, they are constantly interpreting what things mean and responding accordingly. Consider the simple case of a person crossing a street. As outside observers, we might observe that a person remains stationary until the image of an outstretched hand is replaced by the image of a person crossing the street. Is this a case of the person's behavior being determined by an external stimulus or is this a case of the person interpreting objects and then choosing a course of action? A quantitative researcher might regard this as an example of stimulus-response behavior with a conditioned response to the change in images. A qualitative researcher, on the other hand, regards this behavior as an example of meaningful interpretation followed by a purposeful course of action. And how does the qualitative person know this? He asks the pedestrian to describe how he accomplished this everyday task of crossing the street.

WORLDS OF MEANING

At the center of explanations for human behavior is the concept of "meaning." Understand the meaning(s) and you'll understand the behavior, because behavior follows meaning. Meaning may be shared among individuals: Two or more people (or even two cultures) can agree upon what something means. Meaning can also be idiosyncratic, peculiar to one person. Qualitative researchers seek out shared meanings in order to discover patterns of human behavior. An automobile, of course, is not just a means of transportation. It can also be—all at the same time—an expression of self to an individual, an expression of self to others, an investment, a feeling of freedom, a sensory experience, a means of escape, and an expression of concern for others or for the environment.

Meaning is not static; it changes over time and place, within context, and with people. Something you have accomplished may have one meaning for you at the time of the accomplishment; 10 years later it may have a different meaning. The accomplishment may be more or less important to you. The accomplishment hasn't changed at all, but the meaning of the accomplishment has.

FROM THE PARTICIPANT'S PERSPECTIVE

In the world of qualitative research, researchers believe that to understand behavior you must be able to uncover the meaningful objects in people's worlds and understand those objects from the perspective of the people being studied. Any given product may have one meaning for the producer, another for distributors, and yet others for different groups of consumers. What does it mean to buy and use a certain product category? Within the product category, what kinds of meanings do the various brands or offerings have? How do these meanings lead to or connect to decisions to buy certain brands and not others? These are the kinds of questions that qualitative researchers attempt to answer.

By asserting that meaning arises from within the person, qualitative researchers deny that meaning can exist in the object. Product consumption and brands have no meanings except for those that consumers are willing to give them. And this meaning is multiple, individual, shifting, contextual, and shared.

By the turn of this century, smoking cigarettes had taken on a very different meaning than it had in the 1950s. Although there may have been product improvements during the last half of the last century, smoking moved collectively in our judgment from socially acceptable to socially and individually irresponsible. Smoking itself did not change; the meanings, the interpretations—the reality of smoking—did, and changes in behavior followed.

MULTIPLE TRUTHS

In a qualitative world, there is no single, determinable truth. Instead there are truths to be found, and these truths are bound by the time, the context, and the individuals who believe them. What constitutes truth is often shared beliefs or shared realities. That Brand X is the best cleaning product is a truthful statement within the time, context, and individuals who believe it. That the world is flat was true within the time, context, and individuals who believed it.

Obviously, the external world does not allow just any interpretation of it; there are limits, often defined by culture. However, the limit to interpretations is not "1"; it is a much greater number. Suppose at the end of a business lunch your potential employee took a piece of bread and pushed it in a circular motion about the surface of his dinner plate, soaking up the last juices of the entree, and then proceeded to eat it. This practice, called sopping, would carry a certain meaning in an American restaurant, probably that the candidate possessed few social skills and lacked a basic knowledge of dining etiquette. However, the same, exact behavior in a restaurant in France would be seen as perfectly normal and acceptable. Shift the location to many American supper tables and it remains acceptable. Meaning changes with context.

Qualitative Words

Within the qualitative research tradition, certain words carry great significance and meaning. In other traditions, the persons who participate in a research study are commonly called *subjects* or *respondents*, suggesting a hierarchical relationship between the researcher and others. Qualitative researchers want to narrow the distance between themselves and others and therefore prefer the term *participants* to refer to the individuals who assist by providing information to the researcher.

Theory in qualitative research refers to an organizing scheme for the data that places them in orderly patterns and gives meaning and insight into the lives of others. Theory is not posited before data collection; it comes out of the data and is thus referred to as *grounded theory* because it is grounded in the data (Glaser & Strauss, 1967).

Guesses and suppositions about what the researcher may find are called *working hypotheses* and are altered and revised or cast aside as data collection proceeds.

Triangulation refers to the use of multiple perspectives, multiple methods, multiple research sites, and multiple researchers to understand more fully the object of the investigation. Multiple approaches are always preferred.

The Qualitative Approach

Qualitative researchers begin with inductive analysis and then often swing back and forth between inductive and deductive analyses. To start inductively means that researchers find objects and attempt to identify and classify them by their characteristics or distinguishing features. An object can be a physical object such as a chair, a cultural belief such as "time is limited," or a guiding principle such as "work hard to get ahead." Then the qualitative researcher moves to the next object and compares it to what has already been defined, asking if the new object fits within the category already established or if it demands a new category. The researcher continues in such fashion until all such categories are defined and the relationships that exist between the categories are established.

Assume that you encounter a spherical-shaped object of orange-yellow color. You note that it grows on a tree. It has a puckery skin that you can peel off. The inside is softer, more watery than the outside, and it has a pleasing taste. You might label this "tasty sphere." Next you notice another spherical-shaped object of about the same size resting under the tree. It has a white, leathery skin that can be removed with great difficulty. It fact, the skin appears to have been sewn on. You remove the skin and find yards and yards of string wrapped around a hard center. The center is black, and when you bite it you discover it is not juicy or soft and has a most unpleasant taste. Is this also an example of a tasty sphere, or are the differences so great as to demand a new category? That depends on the skill of the researcher. Are oranges and baseballs in the same category? Only if we define the category as "spherical-shaped objects." But in this case, shape is not the essence of the category, and we know that because we went beyond a surface-level investigation. One of the tasks for the qualitative researcher is to go beyond surface descriptions to understand the essence of the world as constructed by the participants.

Qualitative researchers want to know the categories of meaning that participants use in everyday life, but discovering them, categorizing them, and charting their relationships is a little more difficult than being able to distinguish oranges from baseballs.

Qualitative Methods

Qualitative research methods are diverse and varied. Any method that allows the researcher to capture the worlds of others can be a valid qualitative technique. These include observation, participant observation, in-depth interviewing, documents, and record analysis. Qualitative researchers rarely rely on a single method of gathering data because each method brings its own biases.

Participant observation is sometimes regarded as the purest qualitative research technique because it requires the researcher to spend extended time in a participant's natural setting observing and learning how to do things the way the participant does things. Want to know what it's like to work on a production line in a factory? One of the ways to do that is to observe people on the line, listen to them talk about working on the line, and spend some time on the line yourself.

Participant observation is time-consuming and expensive, and there are many situations where access to observing can't be negotiated. If you wanted to study what remedies people take when they have headaches, a pure participant observation approach would require you to participate and observe individuals until the onset of a headache. This could take several days or weeks of observation before a participant suffers a headache. A more economical approach—but perhaps a less rich one—would be to conduct interviews with consumers regarding when and how headaches occur, what remedies they take, and whether specific remedies are associated with certain kinds of headaches.

You might also convene a group of known headache sufferers and engage them in a group discussion.

Qualitative Data

Qualitative researchers eschew structured questionnaires and scaling devices because they present the world as constructed by the researcher. A series of statements drawn from the research literature or previous studies presents a view of reality as collected by the instrument writer. Any qualitative research technique will allow for participants to respond in their own words. Thus, it is possible to have a qualitative survey in which respondents have the opportunity to introduce their worlds, not respond to the researcher's view of the world.

Almost anything can count as data in a qualitative study. This includes letters, shopping lists, photographs, memos, diaries, essays, audiotaped and videotaped interviews, and group discussion transcripts. Because the planner is looking for anything that can give him insight into the meaningful worlds of his participants, anything that can do that should be used.

Qualitative researchers prefer to use multiple methods and multiple sources of data because any given method of data collection and analysis carries its own biases and weaknesses. Through triangulation planners hope to get a fuller or more nearly complete understanding of consumers by drawing from multiple sources of data and using multiple techniques.

Analysis of Qualitative Data

Every qualitative researcher is allowed to be his own theorist. Rather than going into a study with a theory to be tested, qualitative researchers try to enter the worlds of others without any presuppositions about what they might find. Doing qualitative research requires planners to set aside their own personal biases and to be fully open to understanding the world as constructed by others.

Assume that your agency has a federal contract to investigate why teenage mothers on welfare continue to have additional children, and it's up to your agency to develop message strategies that would encourage teen mothers not to have additional children.

Your job as a qualitative researcher is neither to pass judgment on your participants nor to inject your own personal opinions as to why this happens. Your goal is to enter into the world of teen mothers (through observation, interviews, participation, etc.) and to understand the meaning of "children" as the teen mothers construct that meaning. You might have a number of working hypotheses that initially guide your collection of data, but you'll most likely discard or alter these as you begin to collect data. For example, you might wonder beforehand whether

- teen mothers have additional children because they are not knowledgeable about their bodies and birth control methods
- teen mothers have additional children as a way of trying to maintain a relationship with a partner who may provide financially for the children
- teen mothers have additional children as a way of gaining additional welfare dollars for their families
- teen mothers have additional children as a way of increasing their status within the community in which they live
- teen mothers have additional children because of peer and social pressures that encourage procreation during the teen years

Each of these five working hypotheses may offer no explanation, a partial explanation, or (rarely is this the case) the complete explanation. Getting at the meaning of additional children to these mothers requires that you understand the world in which they live as they understand it so that message strategies or programs discouraging a behavior can be developed. Your own personal biases and opinions are of no value here, unless, of course, you have a history of being an unwed teenage mother on welfare. Then your own personal experience and insight can be extremely valuable to you. However, planners should never assume that because they are also members of the group being studied that their experiences are the same. No two people have exactly the same experience and thus don't understand the world in exactly the same way.

The basic question for most qualitative researchers is, "What is going on here?" Any method of inquiry and any method of data analysis that can help to answer that question should be considered an acceptable one. Naturally, there is rarely, if ever, just one thing going on. Human behavior is highly complex, and more commonly the planner will find that multiple things are going on. For example, the question, "What is going on inside the supermarket?" has multiple answers. In fact, the number of answers to what is going on is probably equal to or greater than the number of people inside the supermarket. Some people are at the cash register, scanning packages, taking other people's money, and putting their purchases in bags. Other people are pushing carts, pausing temporarily at different locations, and then deciding whether to place certain items in the cart, sometimes putting items in and then taking them out of the cart and putting them back on the shelf. Some people have lists of items that they consult frequently, and others have no list at all. Some people have many items in their carts, and when the cart is full, they stand in one kind of line. Others seem to have only a few items that they carry in their hands and they stand in another kind of line. Yet other people are placing items on the shelves and others are handing out product samples. If we asked the persons mentioned what they were doing, we would probably get answers such as shopping for the week, dropping in after work, running in and out, checking out, waiting, checking people out, bagging, re-stocking, and sampling—all of which are part of a smooth-flowing super-market operation.

Because they enter the world of others without preconceived notions about how things are, qualitative researchers often use the term *sensitized concept* rather than theory. Grounded theory (Glaser & Strauss, 1967) means that any explanation you have is grounded in and comes out of the data, not before data are collected. A sensitized concept is one that's sensitive to and comes out of the data. Common everyday sayings such as, "It's not what you know, but who you know," and "Who you are determines the quality of service you get" are in fact theories about how the social world works grounded in people's everyday experiences.

CODING PARADIGMS

No two researchers will approach data analysis in exactly the same way.

Some planners prefer to do the analysis by hand, working from paper copies of transcripts that they mark up, cut up, rearrange, and put back together in various ways. Other planners prefer to work at the computer, inserting word codes, highlighting texts, inserting comments, and so forth, using a simple word processing program. Still others prefer to use a specialized computer program such as NUD*IST (Qualitative Solutions and Research, 1997) to help them develop their codes and manage their data.

Coding data and using coding paradigms are two ways of reducing data to manageable and meaningful units. Keep in mind that data analysis and coding should begin at the same time as data collection. In survey research, all of the data are collected, usually entered into a data analysis program, and then analyzed.

In qualitative research, data collection and tentative analysis occur simultaneously. If you wait until all of your transcripts are complete and then try to begin analysis, you have created an almost unmanageable task for yourself.

Analysis itself can be a long, demanding process. Most researchers will swing back and forth between data collection and data analysis as they complete the research assignment. In fact, it is your own understanding of the phenomenon you're studying that tells you when it is time to stop collecting data.

Strauss and Corbin (1998) suggest a coding paradigm that consists of coding data into (a) the phenomenon, (b) conditions, (c) actions/interactions, and (d) consequences. The phenomenon is a repeated pattern of behavior and commonly is the behavior you're trying to understand. A condition is a complex set of events that lead up to the phenomenon. Actions/interactions represent the ways (or strategies) people use to respond to the phenomenon. Consequences represent the end result of the actions/interactions. This coding paradigm is particularly useful when coding for a process, such as decision making. Planners often assume that "buying" or "decisions to buy" are the central phenomena of their studies. When this is the case, the planner might examine the data looking for (a) conditions that lead to purchase (natural depletion, wearing out, running out, acute need, emergencies); (b) actions/interactions involved in the buying decision (gathering information, making price comparisons, asking a friend, looking for information on the World Wide Web (WWW), visiting a retail location); and (c) consequences (satisfaction, dissatisfaction, unexpected benefits, repeat purchase, depleting the savings account, prideful ownership).

Using a coding paradigm created by others can be very handy in the initial coding stages because it makes you look at the data in different ways and may allow you to see relationships within the data that are not obvious. The Strauss and Corbin paradigm is especially helpful when coding for process and when coding for the duality of structural features (often the conditions) and action.

However, planners should not be reluctant to develop their own coding paradigms. Some researchers, for example, are content to code for major themes or trends in the data without charting the relationships among the themes. For example, a study of the current buying patterns among teenagers might include fashion trends, eating-out patterns, musical tastes, activities with friends, and part-time work. There may or may not be a relationship among the various themes (a pure qualitative researcher will believe there is!), and it may be that only one or two dominant themes are of interest to the client. In such cases, the planner may be satisfied to stop with a thematic analysis.

Still other planners may wish to do a metaphorical analysis of the words that participants use. Metaphors take the characteristics of one thing and associate them with something entirely different; they are powerful ways of making intangible concepts more tangible. By talking about a thing in terms of something else in an effort to make it more comprehensible, metaphors can be used to provide powerful insight into how people think of themselves and how they behave (Felton, 1994). Consider this quote from a corporate trainer:

> I just can't seem to get through everything I need to in the time we have. There're always so many people interrupting me with questions and making me lose my place. I'm very frustrated with not being able to finish the training session on time.

To code for metaphors, we ask how the language and expressions used by the participant reflect other figures or jobs. The participant says he "can't get through . . . on time," "interrupting me," "losing my place," "not able to finish on time." Obviously, the trainer sees himself as someone who must adhere to a fixed schedule on time, have no interruptions, maintain a train of thought, and finish on time. Metaphorically, the participant's language is based in transportation. More listening on our part might help to establish the means of transportation: Is he an Amtrak engineer speeding down the train(er's) track? An airline pilot on his way from New York to Los Angeles? A captain of a cruise ship? These types of insights into how people see themselves can help us to understand their worlds.

Metaphors exist within the language but slightly below the surface level. Most are usually not visible to the persons who speak them. Nonetheless, they sometimes pop out at the planner and can be a useful analytical tool.

GETTING IT RIGHT

If human behavior is as complicated as qualitative researchers believe, how is the planner ever to know if she has gotten it right? Unfortunately, there is no simple test or assessment that can confirm the validity of an interpretation. However, there are some procedures and safeguards that planners can use to reduce the chances that they got it wrong.

First, planners have to accept that it is impossible to produce an interpretation of people's behavior that is a verisimilitude, or exact copy, of human behavior. The best you can produce is a reasonable interpretation that appears to explain the behavior. Before entering a research setting, planners should ask themselves (through working hypotheses) what they think is going on. If the answer after the research is the same as before, the planner has probably gotten it wrong: Rather than discovering a pattern of behavior, the planner has imposed her own interpretation on the data. Keeping track of your own personal biases, prejudices, and opinions before and during the research process helps to guard against their overly influencing your interpretation of the data. It's a good idea to write these down beforehand.

During the data collection and temporary analysis of data, planners can write memos or notes to themselves, expressing their initial reactions and conclusions. Tracking these during the research process can help you to determine if you have come to understand others or if you have imposed your own interpretations on the data.

Asking a colleague or team member to determine if your interpretations are reasonable based on her examination of some of the transcripts and your coding scheme is another way to guard against personal bias. Particularly in a team research situation, all team members must come to a shared understanding of what the data mean.

Yet another way to guard against personal bias is to take your interpretations back to your participants and ask them if they agree. In the process of analysis, you should write summaries of your thoughts on the interviews you're conducting. Ask the participants to read the summaries of their interviews to see if your interpretation of the interview matches the participant's perspective.

In the final analysis, it's not so much whether you understood all of the behavior you may have observed or listened to people talk about, but whether you have a sufficient understanding to speak to the client on behalf of your research participants. Can you provide a reasonable description of the world of the people you have studied from their perspective(s)? If so, you have accomplished your research task as a planner.

Summary

Qualitative researchers see individuals as active, interpreting beings who construct worlds of meaning and act upon the world rather than allowing the world to act upon them. Qualitative research seeks to see and to understand the world from the perspective of the people they study.

Meaning is a central concept in qualitative studies because meaning and interpretation guide behavior. Meaning is said to be multiple, changing, and dependent on context and time.

Qualitative researchers prefer to use multiple research methods because of the inherent bias in any given method. Data can be analyzed in a variety of ways, including process analysis, thematic analysis, and metaphorical analysis.

Researchers guard against personal bias in their interpretations of human behavior by articulating their own biases before the research begins, by tracking their interpretations as they change, by asking colleagues to review their interpretations, and by sharing their interpretations with their participants.

Qualitative research turns many of the so-called standard research procedures upside down. Getting close to consumers, making them partners in the research process, and massaging data are not research crimes within the qualitative research traditions. The following chapter on ethnographic methods reveals some ways to get close to your consumers so you can understand them better.

Key Terms

Analytic induction: Beginning with a single observation, comparing it to a second observation to find the similarities shared by the two observations, and then continuing to a third and so forth.

Context: The surroundings or environment in which a phenomenon occurs. Context changes the meaning of the phenomenon.

Data: Anything created or changed by humans that gives the researcher insight into how the participants construct their realities

Deductive approach: Procedure that begins with a broad, general statement about relationships that you hope to find

Grounded theory: Theory that is grounded in the data

Inductive approach: Procedure that begins with focusing on a single observation

Metaphor: A way of understanding the essence of something not well understood by comparing it to something more readily understood

Participants: People from whom the researcher gathers information

Phenomenon: Something that becomes the central focus of a research study, often not obvious at the beginning of a qualitative study

Reality: What is perceived to be true by an individual or by groups of individuals. Reality exists within the meaning structures created by the individuals and not in the objects of the physical world. Reality is not static; it changes across time, space, context, and with individuals.

Sensitized concept: A concept sensitive to the data that helps to explain relationships found in the data

Theory: The organizing scheme that helps you to make sense of your data. It grows out of the analytical process; it is not posited before.

Working hypothesis: A researcher's hunch about what he or she may find. Hypotheses are discarded or changed as additional data support or fail to support them

Exercises

1. Talk to 8 or 10 of your friends about their favorite item of clothing. Ask them to talk about how they acquired it, how long they have had it, where and when they wear it, and what makes it special to them. What insights can you draw from the conversations about the meaning of clothes? Is the meaning in the item or in the person? Can you find instances where interaction with others has reinforced or changed the meaning? Are there differences in your understanding between participants who were wearing or able to show you the item compared to those who could only describe it? Does the context in which the person wears the item change the meaning in any way? How can these insights be used to develop message strategy for (a) a laundry detergent that claims to work gently on colors and fibers, (b) a dry cleaning business, (c) a clothing alteration business, or (d) the introduction of a vintage line of clothing?

2. Ask several people to tell you about items they have inherited (or hope to inherit) from a relative. Ask them to tell you about what they think the item meant to the relative and what it means to them. How has the relative's owning the item influenced the meaning of the item for the person who now owns it?

Related Reading

Denzin, N., & Lincoln, Y. (Eds.). (2000). *Handbook of qualitative research* (2nd ed.). Thousand Oaks, CA: Sage.

Glaser, B., & Strauss, A. (1967). *The discovery of grounded theory.* Chicago: Aldine.

Taylor, S. J., & Bogdan, R. C. (1984). *Introduction to qualitative research methods: The search for meanings* (2nd ed.). New York: John Wiley.

3

Ethnographic Methods for Advertising Research

B efore we dive into methods, we need to get a handle on the term *ethno-graphy*. *Ethnos* is a Greek term that denotes a people, race, or cultural group (Smith, 1989). Ethnography is the study of people and the cultures they create. It is a branch of descriptive anthropology devoted to describing ways of life and humankind (Vidich & Lyman, 2000). This sounds a lot like what planners do. In fact, we think of planners as ethnographers. Our job is to be constantly curious about ways of life and humankind. We have to understand people and the culture within which they live. This culture is the context in which our brand, message, and media strategies must resonate.

Getting Emic

There are two general traditions of ethnographic analyses, etic and emic. Etic analyses are views of a culture from outside the culture. In *Why We Buy: The Science of Shopping*, Paco Underhill (2000) describes many etic methods of studying shopping behavior. For example, trailing shoppers is one such method his researchers employ. Trailing involves following shoppers and taking notes about their behavior without being noticed by the shopper. Certainly you can learn a great deal about behavior from watching. However, what you miss from just watching is how individuals make sense of what they are doing. Underhill comments, "in addition to measuring and counting every significant motion of a shopping trip, the trackers must also contribute incisive field notes describing the nuances of customer behavior, making intelligent inferences based on what they've observed" (p. 15). Making such inferences on behalf of your subjects is what an etic analysis is. An etic ethnographic analysis amounts to our interpretation of another's culture.

There is one major pitfall of etic analysis. Consider our researcher stumbling upon a strange custom among a strange people. She deduces that this must be some type of tribal mating dance. After all, each person from the strange culture she is observing engages in a similar dance when passing by the observation point, and both genders are present when this strange motion occurs. But without stopping to ask the participants what's going on, she won't know that this dance is really the result of bare feet on hot pavement.

The second type of ethnographic analysis is emic analysis, or analysis of a culture from within the culture. Emic analysis matches more closely with our perspective on qualitative research. Because culture is created by the participants, we feel it is vitally important to understand the culture as the participants understand it. Also, our marketing messages must resonate within the culture of our participants. Resonance happens when we strike a chord in consumers; when we make them see our products or services in a way that is meaningful in their lives. Resonance happens in the brains of our participants. All of these ideas require making sure we have research methods that give us access to our participants' thoughts and feelings so we can understand how they create their world.

Ethnographies are holistic and attempt to examine a wide variety of ways in which people express the meaning of the culture they are creating. Expressions of meaning can be words, music, literature, diaries, art, dance, mode of dress, construction of personal space, construction of workspace, home décor, architecture and placement of buildings, and so on. Thus, ethnographies usually consist of a variety of data-gathering techniques. They also can be time and cost intensive if done exhaustively.

The good news is that you don't necessarily have to execute a full-blown ethnography to generate ethnographic insights. In fact, many times getting quality ethnographic insights doesn't have to cost a lot of money at all. This chapter explores a few ethnographic methods that can help planners see how people understand the world around them.

Participant Observation

Just about any study that involves humans can be called an observational study. However, participant observation studies require us as researchers to participate to some degree in the thing we are studying. Participant observation is a core ethnographic technique. It's an active technique. It happens in the everyday environment of our consumers. It's a way to experience our consumers' lives firsthand.

Not all subjects can be studied using participant observation. Sometimes topics are too private. We probably wouldn't get too far as participant observers trying to research condom use. Sometimes there is nothing to observe about the topic we are interested in. For example, if we want to understand how people make sense of social issues like advertising potentially harmful products to minors, it's difficult to find something to observe that answers our question. Other times, the context within which the action happens may be unsafe. For example, you want to understand the culture of inner-city gangs but may not be comfortable participating in their activities.

So what types of topics would lend themselves to participant observation? Activities lend themselves well to participant observation. One Tennessee-based planning-driven advertising agency used participant observation to understand the meaning of a state park. Their researchers went camping, sharing the experience of the great outdoors with people who were using the state parks. Want to know how international tourists experience a U.S. amusement park? We did, and we joined a tour bus of French visitors in Orlando, Florida, spending multiple days with them as we all went on vacation. How do people really make a car-buying decision? Find out by going car shopping with prospective buyers.

A major advantage of participant observation is that you get fresh impressions, right as things are happening. You can also see how the experience evolves, how impressions change, how people navigate a situation, and how they relate to others in that situation. With follow-up discussions you can see how people reflect on their experience and make sense of it.

TEENS IN THE MALL

A useful participant observation tool for understanding how people make sense of retail environments is accompanied shopping. That is, you go shopping with consumers. What you do during an accompanied shopping experience depends on the goal of your study. For example, let's say your client is Abercrombie and Fitch (A&F). They are worried that too many teens are buying their clothes, which is making them "uncool" with their core market, college-aged young people. As a brand strategy, A&F is attempting to launch a new line of stores under a different name, directed to teens. In fact, a few test stores are already up and running in some major suburban area malls. Therefore, A&F needs to understand how teens approach the retail environment as well as their specific store. Well, if you've spent any time in a suburban shopping mall, you know teens don't just shop in a mall, they seem to live there—at least during the summer. So what does going to the mall mean to teens? What does buying clothing mean to teens? Well, hang out and do the mall with them. Try to understand how teens make sense of shopping at the new store in the context of the larger experience of going to the mall.

If you were representing a client who markets compact disks, then you would want to go disk shopping with defined types of buyers (e.g., heavy users, medium users, light users). You would probably go to at least two places where your individual subject reports buying CDs. This would allow you to have the participant compare retail environments for you. You can also see how your shoppers navigate a store, what sections they go to first, how they search for CDs, if they use the listening bars, etc. In addition, you can gather thoughts and feelings as the activity is in progress.

Accompanied shopping is an interview on the move. For our disk buyer, we might ask questions like, "What is your impression of this store? Where would you start your search? How do you decide what to look for? What is it like to shop here?" Sometimes projective types of questions can be fun and insightful. For example, if this store were a person, what would that person be like? (We discuss projective techniques in detail later on in Chapter 5).

If possible, we would want to tape record the conversation, which means we need a small portable tape recorder, a remote microphone, a note pad, and good ears. Taking photos can also be useful if the store will allow that. Sometimes taping isn't possible. That means you need those good ears and an even better memory. Whether you can tape while moving or not, build in time for a discussion over coffee or a soda after the shopping experience and have the participant reflect on his day with you. Recording and note taking may be easier in this environment.

Hint: Before charging into a retail store with tape recorder, camera, and notepad in hand, you may want to fill the store manager in on what you're up to. Otherwise you might find yourself being chased from the store by a very large and unsympathetic security guard.

General Issues With Participant Observation Studies

Once you've found a topic that lends itself to participant observation you may need to ask yourself how far you're willing to be a participant. Your G-string client may be very important to your agency, but are you willing to participate as a G-string—clad entertainer to understand the experience of using the product? The good news is that you can understand culture without "going native," or becoming a full participant in the culture. In fact, keeping a bit of distance while within the context of what you are studying can help you see things that might be missed if you are into the culture too much. Instead of actually becoming performers, we can gain emic insight into the culture by spending time in clubs, watching interactions between the audience and the performers, talking with club patrons about the experience of watching the performers, getting to know the performers, gaining access backstage to see what their life is like behind the scenes, listening to their conversations, engaging them in interviews about things specific to our client's products, gaining valuable insights, and avoiding personal overexposure!

GAINING ACCESS AND BUILDING TRUST

Perhaps the two most important steps in fielding an ethnographic study are gaining access to the context you want to study and building trust with your participants. The more public the space in which the phenomenon happens, the easier it is to gain access to it. For example, understanding fan behavior at a sporting event is relatively easy in terms of access. Getting behind the doors of a business to observe how business people make use of technology in the workplace can be a bit more difficult. Getting into homes can be most difficult. Each context requires you to seek permission from different people.

In all cases, we'd recommend that you get permission from your participants. They will want to know why you're around, so you should be up-front about your purpose. Honesty from you is more likely to result in honesty from them than if they are suspicious of your presence. For businesses, you'll need to find out who within the business can give you permission to get in the door. It may be useful to have that person show you around the business setting and introduce you to people to give you more credibility with your participants.

One way to gain access is to go into situations where you have existing contacts. If people know you already and know that you're reputable, you will have an easier time of gaining access. In situations where you do not have existing contacts, use of others who do have contacts is often essential. For example, in a study to develop HIV/AIDS education and prevention strategies for young adults living in rural areas, a team of "city slicker" researchers was faced with the task of gaining access to the everyday lives of rural young adults. We did not know anyone in the target market who lived in the areas we were studying, and we could not find researchers anywhere with contacts in this market. We spent the first few days of the study just exploring the area, looking at businesses, finding out where the schools and churches were, listening to local radio, reading the local newspaper, and just trying to figure out what people did in this area. We knew we needed some local people who would buy into our research project, were knowledgeable about people living in the area who fit our target market, and whom people in the area trusted. We hoped these key people would vouch for us with the locals to help us gain access.

While driving around we noticed that there was only one pharmacy in town. The mental wheels started turning. We thought that at some point just about everyone in a small town is going to need a prescription filled, and the town was small enough that a local pharmacist would likely know many, many people. A pharmacist would be sympathetic to research aimed at a public health issue. Plus, people would likely trust the pharmacist. We knew we had it! But to be on the safe side we stopped several places and told people we needed to fill a prescription. We asked folks where we should go and if they thought the pharmacist would be helpful. Fortunately, everyone we asked seemed to have a great deal of respect for the husband and wife pharmacists who ran the local shop. We drove straight to the pharmacy. After talking with the pharmacists for just a few minutes, we knew we had indeed hit it. They invited us to their home that evening, fed us, and we talked about the project. Immediately they began to help us identify people to use in the study, made contacts for us, and told folks that we were OK.

Having someone to vouch for you is helpful in gaining trust. However, the burden of gaining trust eventually falls on your shoulders. You have to look and sound credible, but not threatening.

In terms of looking credible, think about your audience. If you need to speak with corporate executives, you'd better look like an executive. If you're talking to young adults, blue jeans may be the ticket to reducing barriers between you and your participants.

In terms of sounding credible but not threatening, we've found two techniques that work well. First, let your participants know what you are doing and why. Explain to them that there are no right or wrong answers. Tell them you are there to learn from them. Stress that they are the experts, not you.

The second way to put your participants at ease is to have them talk about the one thing they know best, themselves. Ask them to explain their daily routine to you. The amount of time you spend engaged in this type of conversation depends on the type of person you are talking with. The rapport-building stage is important with executives, but because their time is very valuable you may want to do less of this. If people seem really uncomfortable with you, then you may need to spend more time with this activity.

A word of caution—unless you're an Oscar-winning actor, don't try to be someone you're not. This is especially important with kids. Kids know you're not a kid. You will likely come across pretty goofy if you try to act too much like a kid. Just be yourself. After all, that's what you're asking your participants to be, so why not set a good example?

SNOWBALLING AND LUCK

One strength of ethnographic methods is emergent design. Emergent design means that we can change the research methodology in the field if we find we are barking up the wrong tree or if we find aspects of the culture we haven't yet considered. Randomized participant selection isn't a goal. Rather, pushing for diversity of perspectives regarding the culture you are interested in is a more appropriate goal. In our rural young adults study example, once we gained access to a few young adults, we used them to direct us to other types of people who might be similar or very different from them. This technique of using current participants to recruit additional participants is called "snowballing" and is a useful emerging design tool. We listened to how the young adults described the different types of young people who lived in the community, then asked them to put us in touch with other young people who fit in the various categories of people they had described.

During the ongoing recruiting process, constantly ask yourself, "Whose perspective are we missing?" In our HIV study we expanded our sample to include school administrators, teachers, preachers, preacher's wives, some parents, and so on, and we thought we had it all wrapped up. Then we had a stroke of luck that we couldn't have anticipated. After being stood up for an interview session (which will sometimes happen to the best of us) we wandered around a park in the downtown area of the little town. It was midmorning on Saturday and we noticed a group of young adults cleaning up the park. We walked over, struck up a conversation, and found that these young folks were doing community service for various legal offences. We asked a few if they would talk with us after they were done. Dumb luck led us to an entirely different side of this rural area, a side that our other helpers were not familiar with. Among these young people were folks who represented high school dropouts and who largely fell within a lower socioeconomic category. In fact, upon further discussion with our medical advisors on the study, we learned that women in this particular group are most at risk for HIV infection. We had located what was perhaps the most critical population to find, by being in the field, keeping our eyes open, and asking questions.

WHAT SHOULD YOU BE LOOKING FOR?

What you're looking for in an ethnographic study depends on the research questions. At the very least, to get an emic understanding of the culture you're going to need interview data. We devote an entire chapter to interviewing later on in this book. Beyond that, think about how you're going to make this culture come to life for your client, account team, media planners, and creatives. As a planner, you're lucky. You get to experience this wonderful, rich experience firsthand. Now you have to convey this experience to others. Here are some things you can do:

- Take photos of your participants so your agency and client can put faces to research results
- Take photos of your participants' homes, work places, etc.
- Have your participants help you make a photo essay of a particular experience, like being in a state park
- Have your participants help you make a video essay of an experience
- Have your participants keep a diary of their experiences with you
- Make note of the music, television, films, books, and more, that are popular with your participants
- Whenever possible, use your participants' own words to describe their experience

Let others see your participants' faces and hear their voices. After all, your participants are the experts here. You're the medium. We talk more about presenting your research insights in Chapter 7, "Briefing the Team: Writing and Presenting the Creative Brief."

HOW DO YOU KNOW WHEN YOU'VE RECRUITED ENOUGH PARTICIPANTS?

In ethnographic investigations, as in other types of qualitative studies, data collection and data analysis happen concurrently. If you're not reflecting on the data you are collecting, you cannot know where to go next in the field. You know you have enough participants when you've pushed for diversity among your sample, and you're confident that you're hearing the same variety of perspectives over and over. This is called reaching information saturation or data redundancy.

BUILDING TRUST AND THE OBSERVER EFFECT

No matter what type of research you do, you can't avoid impacting the phenomenon. What you can do is try to lessen your impact on the phenomenon. In participant observation, time and trust can reduce the observer effect. That is, people are likely to act differently if they know they are being observed. However, over time and as your research subjects' comfort level with you rises, more usual behavior tends to emerge.

Some researchers may argue that you can totally overcome the observer effect by going covertly into the research setting. We have major ethical problems with this idea. First, we firmly believe people have the right to know their behavior is being monitored. Also, there is a major risk to your monetary and time investment in the study if you are found out. That is, if people feel their trust has been violated, they are likely to withdraw from you and not give you access to the information you need. Let's face it, without people to research you can't generate emic understandings to guide your strategy. Finally, with skill and patience, the observer effect can be effectively minimized, thus allowing honest flow of information from your participants.

EXITING THE FIELD

By the end of an ethnographic study, you may have spent a great deal of time with your participants. Thinking about how you are going to exit the research setting is important for several reasons. First, later on you may find the need to reenter the setting, so leaving on good terms is essential. Second, you're dealing with human beings who have given you their time and bared their souls to you. What have you given them? Of course, in many of our research initiatives, we depend on monetary compensation to help recruit participants. Although money helps, there are some nonmonetary ways to compensate participants for their efforts. For example, depending on the constraints of the study, debriefing your participants on what you've found out in the study can provide a sense of closure. Your participants are likely to be curious about what you've discovered, and a debriefing can also show them how they've contributed to your knowledge. A debriefing can also be a good validity check for your analysis. If you're getting very curious looks from your participants as you tell them all about their culture, you probably need to ask some more questions. On the other hand, laughs of recognition can send you home from the field with confidence that you've done a decent job of capturing these people's experience.

Sometimes, depending on your topic, you may feel a greater need to give back to your participants. In the HIV study we've been discussing, it was very apparent that many of our participants held beliefs and were engaged in situations that put them at risk of contracting the virus. Our silence could have been interpreted by them as validation that they were safe. To satisfy what we felt was our ethical duty, once their participation had concluded we gave participants leaflets about HIV and AIDS as well as phone numbers they could call for help.

Panel Studies

Many times you can't afford the time or money required for an extended in-field ethnographic experience. Panel studies can be a solution. A panel study involves recruiting a group of people and tracking them over time using a variety of techniques. You can schedule individual or group interviews at various intervals over a specified period of time. In between interview sessions, you can have your participants keep diaries, take photos, or make videos of the experience you are exploring. Sometimes you can use telephone or Internet technology to keep track of what's going on. We'll go into greater detail about using Internet technology in the field in Chapter 6, "Qualitative Research Online: Focus Groups and Interviews."

LAUNCHING THE STEAM N' CLEAN

Panel studies can be useful when you are launching a new product. For example, Erich Pagel, the marketing research director for the Bissell cleaning products company, developed a very successful strategy for a new product launch from a meager $1,500 investment in ethnographic research using a panel design.

Because Bissell had an established record with other cleaning products, they knew that women and children were heavy users of their products. With limited time and money, Pagel looked for an organization where women with children could be found. The local PTA proved to be a great answer to his problem. In return for a $1,500 donation to the organization, Pagel was allowed to give a presentation to the PTA and recruited 20 PTA moms to try out the new Bissell product in their homes. The moms kept diaries of their experience of using the product over a 2- to 3-week period. These diaries were complemented with in-home visits by Pagel so he could see the moms using the product in a natural setting.

Although this quick $1,500 project worked for Bissell's situation, Pagel cautions that such

shoestring ethnography isn't for every project. Observational research can be do-it-yourself if business risk is relatively low, if it's a category that the marketer knows well, and if there are few differences across markets or regions. But marketers shouldn't "try this at home" if they're investigating a brand-new category, or require special access to a customer, say, at a store. (Wellner, 2001, p. 39)

CONSUMER DEPRIVATION

Getting fresh insights about very familiar products can be difficult. Many times people have a tough time expressing what something means to them because that thing is such a natural part of their lives. They take such things for granted. In these situations, you may need to force the issue a bit. One effective way to help people realize how important something is to them is to have them go without that something for a period of time. In planning, this is called a consumer deprivation study. One of the best-known consumer deprivation studies led to the initial version of the Got Milk? campaign.

The Got Milk? campaign, designed by Goodby, Silverstein & Partners, was the first campaign to bring about an increase in milk consumption and sales in the 1990s ("Got Milk? California Fluid Milk Processors Advisory Board," 1996). The original campaign was regional in scope and had been initiated by the California Fluid Milk Processors Advisory Board (CFMPAB). The main problem facing CFMPAB was that milk consumption had declined substantially in California during the 1980s and early 1990s by an average of 2% to 3% each year. Reasons behind the decline were consumer concerns about milk's fat content, a feeling that milk was for kids, and an overall boring image for milk in comparison to other beverages, mainly sodas. Past campaigns had attempted to stem declining milk consumption by giving milk a fun, trendy image, and by running advertising that featured healthy-looking people. Though this advertising had been successful in shifting attitudes toward milk (more than 50% of Californians agreed that, "I should drink more milk than I do"), these attitudes were not translating into sales. In approaching the problem, the ad agency recommended targeting frequent milk users. Targeting current frequent users was based on the idea that it is easier to get people to continue what they would normally do than it is to get people to start doing something they haven't done before.

The insight behind the Got Milk? campaign was simple. The only time people ever think about milk is when they need it and it isn't there. How did the planners from Goodby, Silverstein & Partners generate this insight? You guessed it: with a panel study.

Participants were recruited from focus groups. These brave volunteers were asked not to use milk for a week. They were to keep a diary of everything they ate or drank in that time. What.was revealed in discussions with the panel participants about their week without milk, was that certain foods they loved were absolutely impossible to eat without milk. That chocolate brownie or bowl of cereal was unthinkable without milk. These milk drinkers found the experience frustrating and painful.

The advertising was based on creating cravings for those foods that are impossible to eat without milk. Executions started with one of the food items (a cookie or cereal, etc.) for which milk is the essential complement. The twist in the ads was that there was no milk available to accompany the food, so both the food and the heavenly moment were ruined. The success of the initial campaign for the California Fluid Milk Processors Advisory Board prompted the DMI, a national dairy organization, to adopt the campaign as well ("Got Milk?" 1996). At the national level, additional executions were created. In one national execution, hell was presented as an eternity with all the chocolate chip cookies you could eat but no milk.

General Issues With Panel Studies

When considering a panel study, you need to ask yourself a few questions. The first question is, of course, "Is a panel study appropriate?" Panel studies seem to work best when the participants have a defined task like living without milk or trying out a new product or service. Consumers seem capable of making observations of their own behavior, thoughts, and feelings if the task is specific. They generally seem to have a good time doing it as well.

Panel studies can also give you access to settings that would otherwise be difficult to observe. Instead of traveling with business people, a panel of business travelers can give you ethnographic insights into the life of the business traveler. So if the setting you need to observe is difficult to get firsthand access to, a panel study may be appropriate.

Panel studies require a literate audience that can keep records for you. Make sure your participants are capable of observing themselves and reporting those observations.

A second major question is, "What should the composition of my panel be?" That all depends on the nature of the product and your consumers. In the Got Milk? and Steam N' Clean examples, one local panel worked well for each situation because there aren't strong regional differences in product use or the nature of consumers who will use the product. A milk drinker in California is probably very similar to a milk drinker in New York. However, if there are strong regional differences in the use of your product, or if your product is used by diverse consumer segments, you will need to structure your panels accordingly.

How long should a panel study last? For most tasks, 2 or 3 weeks seem to work well. That's enough time for consumers to get accustomed to the task in their everyday lives, but not long enough for consumers to grow tired of the exercise.

Some research companies employ longer panel studies. For example, some cable networks have a regular group of participants who watch and comment on network programming. These panels can last for one or more television seasons. So it is possible to execute longer panel studies. Longer studies may be necessary, depending on the purchase cycle of your product, seasonality, and so on. When you do longer panel studies, there are special issues to consider. First, you will likely experience member drop-out. You will need to decide whether to replace a dropout or just let the group continue with fewer participants. Second, no matter how dedicated the panel member, you will have lapses in record keeping. People get busy, and your project may take on a lower priority for participants the longer the research project runs. Finally, staying with the same panel participants too long may result in "group think" where you lose the ability to generate fresh or unique insights. If panel members stay too long, they can also become corporate insiders and begin to lose their consumer perspective in favor of a business perspective.

Thus far in this chapter we've talked about various research techniques that can help you generate good strategic insights. There is one essential element in all of these techniques that we have to address. That is, it's useless to go to the trouble of conducting research if we aren't ready to listen. Believe it or not, listening is not as easy as you may think.

Getting Ready to Listen

John Winsor, founder of Radar Communication, a Boulder, Colorado-based research firm that specializes in observation research, commented that some people have the impression that research has to be complicated, new and innovative, and expensive. But according to Winsor, those people are missing the point. He claims, "It's not about the research; it's all about listening" (Wellner, 2001, p. 39).

Research and planning require exceptional listening skills. Too many times, focusing on innovative techniques and the pressure to come up with that one great insight on which to build a profitable strategy can get in the way of hearing your consumers. Also, personal experience can aid a planner in developing strategy, but it can interfere with your hearing. Learning to listen takes work. Planners and researchers must prepare themselves to listen.

Before starting to work with ethnographic research, do a little research on yourself. Have someone interview you about your thoughts and feelings regarding your target market. If no one is available to interview you, then try writing down everything you think you know about this market. Who do you think these people are? What do you think their life is like? What do you think they value? What are their greatest joys and fears? What do they like to buy? What music, TV, film, etc., do you think they prefer? How do you feel about this group? Do you like them or dislike them? Do you have issues with what you perceive as their values or beliefs?

Good planning is the culmination of information and experience—all brought together by the planner. It will never be unbiased or objective. That's okay. However, it is useful to understand how your preconceived notions of the target market may impact your interpretation and use of the enthnographic research results. Knowing how you feel can help you bracket off your preconceived notions for a time and enhance your ability to hear how your targeted consumers make sense of their worlds.

This task can also help your account team and creatives understand the biases and assumptions they are bringing to the project. As a planner you not only have to prepare yourself to listen, you have to prepare your account team, client, and creatives to listen as well.

Summary

In this chapter we've established that the overarching goal of ethnographic studies is achieving an emic understanding of our target consumers' lives and the meanings they ascribe to our products and services. Emic understandings are essential if we want to generate strategy that will break through the clutter and be meaningful to our targeted consumers.

Reaching emic understanding requires using ethnographic research techniques. Such techniques range from time-intensive exercises of living with our consumers and experiencing their daily lives firsthand, to participating in specific consumer activities such as shopping. Panel studies can give us ethnographic insights when we don't have the time or money to actively participate in various activities with our consumers.

Now that we've learned about various ethnographic methods, we turn our attention to developing specialized skills you will need in executing a successful ethnographic study. One of the core skills needed to achieve emic understanding is interviewing. Don't be surprised if interviewing isn't as easy as it first seems. Read on to learn why and how to do it better.

Key Terms

Accompanied shopping: A participant observation method in which the researcher goes shopping with consumers

Bracketing: Becoming aware of your preconceived notions of consumers so that you can see how your assumptions may impact your ability to hear consumers

Consumer deprivation: Asking consumers to do without a familiar product in order to assess what the product really means to them

Covert: Going into a research setting without the participants knowing you're researching them. We do not recommend this strategy.

Debriefing: Letting your research participants know generally what you've discovered in the research project. Can serve as a validity check to your analysis.

Diaries: Written and/or photographic accounts of your participants' experiences compiled by your participants over a specified time period

Emergent design: A research design that can change and evolve over the course of a study in order to get the best possible information. This is considered a major strength of qualitative research.

Emic: Analysis from within the culture

Ethnography: The study of people and the cultures they create

Etic: Analysis from outside the culture

Gaining access: Being allowed into a natural setting to conduct research, or being allowed to talk with the people you are interested in researching

Going native: Becoming a full participant in a culture; losing your perspective as a researcher

Information saturation or redundancy: When you're confident that you're no longer hearing new information/perspectives from your participants

Observer effect: The fact that people often change their behavior when they know they are being observed. Time and experience can help you overcome this.

Panel study: A study over time with the same group of people

Participant observation: A type of study in which the researchers actually participate in the phenomenon they are studying

Rapport: Establishing a level of comfort with the people you are researching in order to get honest answers

Resonate: To connect. We want our marketing messages to resonate or connect with the culture of our participants.

Snowballing: A method of recruiting additional research participants based on referrals from current participants

Validity: In qualitative research, validity means representing your participants' understandings of their worlds as best you can.

Exercises

1. Grab a friend and go shopping! Your research questions is, "How do consumers experience their 'favorite store'?" Start by having your participant identify his favorite store. Then go with him for a visit. Have him tell you what it feels like to be in the store. Have him show you where he usually goes first in the store. Ask him what he likes about the experience. Ask him what he would tell others about this store. Watch him interact with sales people. Drain his brain about the store while he's in it! Then go to a place where you can sit down and talk some more. Ask him how the experience of shopping in the store you were just in compares with shopping in other stores. Ask him about behaviors that you observed while you were in the store with him. Play a projective game with him by asking him a question like, "If the store were a person, what would that person be like?" After the conversation, go home and try to convey in writing what the experience of shopping in the store was to your friend. Try to use his own words as much as possible.

2. Got a favorite product? One that's become such a part of your life you take it for granted? Then do without it for a week. Write down every time you miss having that product. When do you

miss it? What do you miss about it? What would you give to have it at that moment? How do you feel without the product? In other words, conduct a consumer deprivation study on yourself. After your weeklong experience, examine your written accounts of living without the product. How can you convey to others what it was like to be without the product? Use accounts from your diary to help you explain the experience to others.

3. What do you know about seniors (people 65 and older)? Write down everything you think you know. Have a friend conduct an interview regarding seniors with you as the interviewee. Who were you thinking of when you were being interviewed or when you were writing your thoughts? What in your experience has led you to your conclusions? Do you think you've accurately captured what it is like to be a senior? Why or why not? What you've just done is conduct a bracketing interview to help you explore your preconceived notions regarding a target market. Getting these ideas out and on paper can help you see how your preconceived notions may impact what you hear when actually researching your target market.

Related Reading

Geertz, C. (1973). *The interpretation of cultures.* New York: Basic Books.

Jorgensen, D. (1989). *Participant observation: A methodology for human studies.* Thousand Oaks, CA: Sage.

Lecompte, M., & Schensul, J. (1999). *Designing and conducting ethnographic research.* New York: Rowman & Littlefield.

4

Listening to Consumers

The Qualitative Interview

Interviewing has become common practice in American life. Reporters interview sources to gather information for their stories. Sports broadcasters interview athletes about how it feels to have just won or lost the big game. Police officers interview suspects to gather information about who may have committed the crime. Human resource workers interview prospective employees. Media talk show hosts interview almost anyone who has a story of 60-seconds duration to tell, and when there is no one left to interview, talk show hosts interview each other about how well their talk shows are going.

Unfortunately, none of these well-known types of interviews has very much in common with what we call the *qualitative interview*. The interview situations listed above are all conducted from the perspective of the person conducting the interview. A newspaper reporter comes across a juicy quote from one source and suddenly needs an opposing quote to give balance to the news story. A broadcast reporter, knowing that she will be allocated only a few seconds of air time for her story, looks for the "sound bite" that will attract attention. The police officer seeks to confirm or destroy the suspect's alibi. In each of these interview situations, the interview itself lasts only a short time and the person conducting the interview has a story or structure that he is trying to confirm. Qualitative interviewing, on the other hand, is conducted from the perspective of the person being interviewed.

Characteristics of Qualitative Interviewing

Interviewing offers the opportunity to delve deeply into the everyday worlds of meanings constructed by participants. Through interviewing, the planner can discover very complex social connections and gain insight into the cultural nuances of the participants' world. Interviewing is totally dependent on gaining access to and cooperation from a small set of participants and on the participants' talking honestly and truthfully with the researcher. Except for highly sensitive product purchases, access to and cooperation from consumers is not usually a barrier. Most people like to talk about their lives, even to strangers. However, the data from qualitative interviews are only as good as the researcher's interviewing skills and her ability to interpret data, both of which are best learned through experience. Qualitative interviews should be conducted in natural settings of extended duration from the participant's point of view.

NATURAL SETTINGS

A qualitative interview is a face-to-face interaction between a researcher and a participant, usually conducted in the location where the behavior of interest occurs. In all qualitative research, natural settings are preferred over artificial ones. A natural setting could be in a tavern or bar, at a grocery store, in an airplane, on a playing field, or standing in the middle of a stream in the Great Smokey Mountains National Park. Qualitative researchers believe in going to where their research participants are rather than bringing the research participants into the researcher's domain. The emphasis on interviewing in a natural setting comes from the qualitative research belief that context is very important in determining meaning. Conducting qualitative research means getting people to talk about what things mean to them, and this is more easily accomplished in the natural setting.

Consider, for example, that you wanted to know the meaning of trucks to pickup truck owners. You could invite truck owners into the corporate research offices to talk about their trucks or you could go to the homes of the truck owners, ride in their trucks with them, and generally get them to talk about their trucks. Sitting in the truck with the owner suggests many contextual cues about ownership that are lacking in a conference room interview. You might observe a number of features about truck ownership that would otherwise escape you. For example, where is the truck parked overnight? Is it left outside while the family car gets the benefit of the garage? Or is the truck parked in the garage? What kind of accessories and items are inside the truck? Is there a gun rack? Are there items dangling from the rearview mirror? Is the truck interior clean or dirty? Who drives the truck (only the owner?) and for what kinds of trips? Who in the family has a personal set of keys to the truck? Observing and asking these types of questions will lead to a deeper, richer interpretation of the meaning of truck ownership.

OF LONG DURATION

A good qualitative interview will usually last from 30 minutes to 2 hours. The exact number of minutes is less important than the fact that the planner gives the participant sufficient opportunity to say all that he can about the item of interest and, equally important, that the researcher has sufficient opportunity to hear all that the participant has to say. Obviously, some participants are more verbose than others; some elaborate greatly upon their answers and others pretty much stick to short, dry answers. Often you'll find that as the interview continues, the participant opens up and is willing to talk more freely. Most people enjoy talking about themselves, about their work, their hobbies, their families, and their possessions. If participants have been told in advance about the topic of the interview, though not necessarily the planner's specific interest, they will talk more freely.

FROM THE PARTICIPANT'S POINT OF VIEW

The goal of most qualitative research is to come to understand the participant's world in the way and in the concepts the participant uses. This is a rather noble and lofty goal, one that's almost impossible to achieve. Nevertheless, it suggests that researchers will not impose a world of meaning (and words) upon the participant's world but will instead seek to understand the meaning that things have in the world of the participant. Often, the researcher will have to assume a naive and uninformed position to be able to really listen to what people are saying.

A common mistake made by beginning qualitative interviewers is to add too much of their own commentary to the interview, thus negating their opportunity to really hear what the participant is saying. Qualitative interviewing is extremely demanding intellectual work. It requires the ability to maintain a single focus of thought for several hours while formulating probes and follow-up questions at the same time. Understanding things from the other person's perspective, or from the insider's perspective, suggests that the interviewer will do very little talking, will refrain from imposing concepts or judgments upon what the participant is saying, and will gently lead the participant through the areas of discussion.

Getting Ready to Interview

PREPARING THE INTERVIEW GUIDE

In getting ready to conduct a series of qualitative interviews, the planner should prepare a discussion guideline of broad topics, moving from the general to the specific. Usually four or five topics or questions are all that can be covered in a single interview. The first question should always be very broad and invite the participant to talk about his life, his work, or his family. In a qualitative world, everything is connected to everything else, and one of your goals as a qualitative researcher should be to uncover those connections. Possessions, brands, buying habits, and choices of where to shop and what to buy are not isolated decisions; they're all connected to other aspects of participants' lives.

If you start the interview with a direct question related to a narrow focus, you'll never uncover these connections. The list of four or five questions will serve as a guide to what you want to hear about, and you'll create most of the direct questions as the interview progresses. Qualitative interviewing asks participants to talk about things they have experienced, so asking participants to conjecture and speculate on things they have not experienced is not likely to yield very reliable information.

An interview guide for cat owners, for example, that sought to understand not only the meaning of the cat to its owner but also why cat owners buy certain brands of cat box filler, or cat food, or cat treats, might consist of the following broad topics:

1. *Family.*   Tell me about your family (spouse, children, grandchildren) and neighborhood (type of housing, neighborhood, neighbors).
2. *Pets.*   Tell me about your family's pets (dogs, birds, fish, snakes, rabbits, cats).
3. *Cats.*   Tell me about the cats that you have (Prompts: cats' names, personalities, types, behavior, care, feeding, where sheltered, toys, whether neutered or spayed, major caregiver).
4. *Cat foods, cat treats, cat care.*   (If the owner has not introduced the topic of interest to the researcher, then the researcher might ask more specifically at this point such questions as: Do you buy cat box filler for your cat? Where is the cat box kept? How often is it changed? Who usually changes it? Who buys the cat box filler? Where do you buy it? What brand[s] do you buy? Have you tried different brands?)

Note that the interview guide moves from general questions to specific questions. By doing so, the researcher hopes to uncover meaningful connections to buying behavior. Does the fact that the neighbor has a fierce dog, for example, lead to certain types of cat confinement that might not occur otherwise? Does the owner feel guilty about leaving the cat alone and therefore compensate by buying more expensive brands for the cat? These are the kinds of connections that can be discovered only through qualitative research.

PREPARING THE DATA SHEET

You should have a data sheet for each participant you interview. On it you should record the participant's name, address, and any other information pertinent to the reason for your study, such as marital status, family size, household type, income, type of job, certain kinds of possessions. You won't be able to think of all possible relevant variables to record, but make a note of those that seem important before you begin the study. Others may arise during the course of the interview, or it may take two or three interviews before you see a connection between what you're interested in and some unforeseen item. For example, it may not be just that a participant is married but rather how long the person has been married that explains certain kinds of behavior.

In addition to a data sheet, most qualitative research will require that you gain the participants' informed consent evidenced by their signatures on consent forms. Such forms usually address a variety of things, including the nature of the research to be conducted; whether the participants are to be paid; what use will be made of the data (usually with the stipulation that none of the participants' names will be attached to the data); any potential harm that may come to the participants; and a clause stating the participants' right to withdraw from the study at their own choosing.

PREPARING THE MECHANICS

Most qualitative interviewers record their interviews with a handheld tape recorder. Condenser microphones can be unreliable, so arrange to have a good-quality external microphone attached to the recorder and always check the volume and make a sample recording in the exact place where you will conduct the interview. For example, if you're interviewing a participant at her kitchen table, you can make small talk with the participant while you set up the recorder. Place the recorder between the two of you but make sure it's off to one side so it doesn't interfere with the direct line of sight between you and the participant. Turn on the recorder and in a normal tone of voice say the date and where you are and the type of interview. Then replay it to make sure you're getting a good quality recording. If you don't—and you later discover that you have left the volume too low or have left the pause button on, or have forgotten to put a tape in—you have lost not only a half-day's work but much valuable information! So take a minute or so and always check the quality of the recording you're getting. Be sure that the microphone is not too close to an air-conditioning unit, for example, or the background noise may obliterate all of the conversation.

Conducting the Interview

For most researchers, the first qualitative interview is a bit disappointing. Many who are accustomed to using a structured interview guide have never really learned to listen to what the participant says. Rather, they're only half listening while thinking of what they are going to say next. As a general rule in qualitative interviewing, what you ask next is always based on what the participant has just said. When you do this, you allow the participant to make and reveal the connections of things rather than imposing your connections upon the participants' words. Once you've completed the data sheet and have asked the participant to talk about himself or herself generally, move to the area that's of interest to you by introducing the topic at one level of abstraction above your item of interest. For instance, if you want to know about truck ownership, start at the level of vehicle ownership or how one gets to and from work, rather than a pointed question about trucks. Let's say that a participant says,

> In this house there's me and my wife. And we have a daughter who's in third grade. She's eight years old and will be nine next June. I work at a window replacement company and my wife's a bookkeeper for an insurance company. We got two dogs and one cat.

Your next question should be related to what the participant just said and moving toward your topic of interest. If your subject is dog food, then you might say, "Tell me about your pets." If the subject is job satisfaction, then you might say, "Tell me about your job." If the subject is marital relationships, you might say, "Tell me about your wife." If the subject is trucks, you might say, "How do you and your wife get to work?" Notice that almost any topic can be pulled from this very brief self-description, but the appropriate one is the one that goes in the direction of the subject of the interview and is still one level of abstraction above the topic. First ask the respondent to talk about the dogs, waiting to see if he introduces the topic of dog food. If he does, you can be fairly sure that he'll reveal how the subject "feeding the dog" or "dog food" is related in his mind to the concept of "dogs."

Regardless of what the participant mentions, some things you absolutely do not way to say are, "I have a dog, too," "My sister worked for an insurance company once," or "I have a daughter." Although rules of polite conversation might suggest that you contribute to the conversation, a qualitative interview is not a two-sided conversation (so be polite, but just don't talk too much). You're not conducting the interview so the participant can learn about you; rather, you're conducting it so you can learn about the participant. Avoid all attempts to interject things about yourself into the conversation, as they will just detract from your concentrating on what the participant is saying. Though most of the situations qualitative interviewers encounter while developing advertising strategy are rather benign and nonthreatening, think about occasions when you might call upon your interviewing skills in the name of developing self-help programs or community programs. In those cases you often want to be absolutely sure that you do nothing to indicate approval of the behavior. Consider this revelation from a woman who physically abused her husband and was ordered to a treatment program: "It's his fault anyway because he ain't much of a man. If he was a real man he wouldn't have let me hit him with the iron skillet." Here you've discovered a rather strange, but nonetheless common, belief among husband abusers: "It's his fault." You'd want to refrain from saying or doing anything that reinforced this belief such as, "Yeah, I would have hit him, too," or "He surely deserved to be hit." In the same way, refrain from approving of the consumption behavior that participants talk about. Your goal is to understand it from the perspective of the participant, not to add your perspective to it. Similarly, consider this revelation from an unmarried, pregnant teenager: "For breakfast I had a bottle of pop and some pig skins." Unless you're providing nutritional advice—and no matter how much you want to chastise the participant for her diet and its possible effects on her unborn baby—you must refrain from making judgments. Approve, and you seemingly condone the behavior. Disapprove, and you greatly diminish the chances that the participant will continue to be open in her answers. Be content to take the role of recorder while you're gathering the information.

As you move from point to point in the qualitative interview, try to pose your questions and prompts in terms of and in relation to what the participant has just said. Avoid asking participants to speculate with "If" and "What if" questions. Rather, ask them to recall or call upon a time in their lives when something did occur. If you want to know if dog owners take their sick animals to veterinarians, it's better to ask, "Has your dog ever been sick?" and proceed from there than it is it ask, "If your dog were sick, would you take it to the veterinarian?" Though the difference is wording is slight, the difference in accuracy may be great. One question asks the participant to tell about something that has happened, the other asks the participant to speculate about something he might do if something did happen. Keep your questions grounded in the real and the concrete.

At some point, the participant may have revealed all that he can about a particular aspect of the subject or the subject itself. At that point, it can be useful to summarize your discussion thus far and ask if anything else occurs to the participant. You might say, for example, "We've talked about your family car and truck, that you drive the truck to and from work, that you use the truck to haul trash and recyclables to the recycling center, that you don't have shelter for the truck but wish you did, that you use the truck when you buy gardening materials and building supplies, that the truck is 'yours' and the car is 'hers' but you take care of the maintenance on both of them, that you drive the car and not the truck to church on Sundays." Then you might ask, "Are there any other places or times when you drive the car but not the truck or drive the truck but not the car?"

Your participant might recall that when it's snowing he drives his wife to work in the truck for safety. Now you have another line of discussion, one dealing with truck safety, and once that's exhausted you can return to prompts regarding appropriate places to drive the truck.

You'll notice that qualitative interviewing does not always proceed in a linear fashion, nor should it. Though you have your list of four or five topic areas to cover, how you get to them is less important than the fact that you do get to them using the concepts and meanings that your participants use.

Sometimes a participant will use a word or phrase that seems to have a special or insider meaning to her. In these cases it is best not to assume that the word means what you think it means but rather to ask the participant to explain it.

For example, a participant, in talking about her husband's trips to the grocery store, revealed, "When I'm not with him, he goes down the potato chip and ice cream aisle." Few, if any, grocery stores stock potato chips and ice cream in the same aisle. So, rather than assuming we understand the participant, it's better to say, "I'm not sure I'm understand. Can you tell me what a potato chip and ice cream aisle is?" In this case, it was any aisle that stocked junk food—but junk food that the wife didn't approve of the husband buying. Words and phrases that have unique meaning to the participants but that are rarely found in a dictionary are called *emic words*. Listen carefully for emic words; they can be very revealing about how participants construct their everyday worlds.

Introducing Objects

Sometimes you will have an object such as a proposed advertisement, a logo, a prototype of a new product, a set of statements, or a description of something that you want the participant to respond to. These items are best introduced at the end of the interview instead of at the beginning or in the middle because they have great power to stunt and skew discussion. If you show participants a proposed advertisement at the beginning of the interview, chances are it will color

and direct most of what they have to say. It's better to listen to what the participants have to say and introduce the commercial at the end. Otherwise, participants may decide that you are really interested only in their opinion of the object.
Placing an object at the end gives both the participant and the researcher a very
rich base from which to evaluate it. In a study about how adult learners decide
to return to school, we interviewed adult learners in depth about the decision-
making process, when they decided to return to school, who had been influen-
tial in their decision, and how long they labored over the decision. At the end
of the interview, participants were asked to judge, in their own terms and words,
the value of a commercial encouraging adult learners to enroll at a particular
school. By the time the commercial was shown, it was quite obvious in each case
that the commercial badly missed the mark. The planners knew not only that the
commercial missed the mark but also had gathered considerable insight into
why it did.

Ending the Interview

When you have properly summarized, in various steps along the way, all that the
participant has told you and the participant has nothing else to say, then it's time
to close the interview. Turn off the tape recorder. Thank the participant for her
time and make arrangements for the participant to be able to contact you in case
she thinks of something else she wants to tell you. Indicate how helpful the participant has been to your research project and ask if she has any questions. Also
ask for permission to follow up with the participant if needed. At this point, look
carefully for any clues from the participant that she may have more to say. For
some participants, turning off the tape recorder and signaling an end to the
interview brings on a greater openness to reveal. This is more likely to be true
when you're interviewing about personally sensitive topics, so don't rush away
from the interview too quickly.

Analyzing the Transcripts

Analyzing qualitative data actually begins at the time you're collecting the data.
Listening carefully to what your participant says and posing your next question
based on what has just been said is an early form of analysis. You begin to see
how concepts are related in the participant's world. Likewise, you should do at
least a cursory analysis of each interview before you proceed to the next one.

Conducting a qualitative interview demands so much concentrated attention that two or three interviews per day is all you should attempt to do. If you're interviewing in a language that is not your native language, be satisfied to do only two interviews per day at most. Otherwise, you'll become so mentally tired that you will miss important details during subsequent interviews.

Your initial analysis might consist of a brief written summary of the interview along with a series of questions that point out potential connections.

Particularly when you're working with other qualitative interviewers, writing memos to yourself and to your research team members is important. Keep in mind that you're trying to discover things that are true for the group of individuals being interviewed, not idiosyncratic meaning for one individual alone. If you have in your mind even a sketchy analysis of your first interview, you'll be able to see some similarities in the second interview as you conduct it.

Even though you may write a summary of each interview, it's still important to prepare a full transcript of each interview. The planner or else a clerical assistant can do this. In either case, it is important that you check the accuracy of the transcription against the recorded tape. An advantage of doing the transcription yourself is that it gives you another opportunity to hear the interview and perform some analysis along the way. It also gives you a chance to critique yourself as an interviewer, asking if you posed appropriate prompts along the way and if you followed all the important lines of questioning. Usually, the less talking you do and the more talking the participant does, the better the quality of your interview. Do a quick line count of the interview. If you were speaking half of the time, you've probably contributed too much. As a rule of thumb, a good interview has the participant talking 80% or more of time. As you become more skilled at interviewing, you'll note that you talk less and listen more.

When do you know you have interviewed a sufficient number of people? This is obviously related to your research purpose and the size of the overall group. However, a point of redundancy usually sets in between the 8th and the 15th interview; that is, when an additional interview reveals no new information, it is time to stop interviewing. Obviously, additional interviews would give you additional examples of the phenomenon you're studying, but it's understanding the essence of the research topic that's most important to you, not collecting as many examples of it as you can.

After you have completed and transcribed the interviews, the really difficult intellectual work begins. Analyzing qualitative transcripts requires an open and creative mind. It requires reading and rereading the transcripts and fully immersing yourself in the text. A helpful starting point is to read through all the transcripts and summaries first and make notes of what relationships seem to exist. If you're studying a process—for example, buying a car—then try to fit things into a time line and ask yourself how the participants' activities changed from recognizing the need to buy a car to the actual purchase.

DEVELOPING A CODING SCHEME

Qualitative researchers view the human world as one of purposeful activity. Individuals encounter objects, situations, and events in their lives. They interpret the meaning of such things and then plan courses of action that fit that interpretation. Individuals are not passive beings acted upon, but rather active individuals going about their daily lives. For this reason, try to code your transcripts by activities such as interpretations, actions, strategies, and the conditions under which these occur. Rather than using passive codes such as "happy" or "sad," make the codes active: "experiencing joy" or "regretting past actions." Seeing individuals as active beings will help you find the connections between their acts—and also the conditions under which these occur and their consequences. Consider that many people, when they are feeling blue, will buy a little reward for themselves to make themselves feel better. We can construct this line of behavior as follows: Experiencing disappointment leads to feeling sad, which leads to buying a product or service, which leads to experiencing upbeat emotions. This is an almost universal buying phenomenon. Some people will buy CDs, others might buy a magazine, a book, perfume, clothing, or treat themselves to a manicure. It is not the physical qualities of the CDs, magazines, books, perfumes, clothing, or manicures that group these products together, but rather the meaning of each product to the individual who purchases it. In a qualitative world, everything is connected to everything else.

Analyzing qualitative data requires you to ask a series of questions about each piece of data you collect. One question it's always useful to ask is, "What is this an example of?" Qualitative analysis begins inductively. The researcher finds an example of something and then tries to match it conceptually to something else. The researcher proceeds in this fashion, adding things, changing the definitions of things, creating new categories, and looking for how categories are connected until he has exhausted all the data.

Consider the following quote from a series of interviews about husband and wife shopping behavior. The wife is talking about how her husband influences her buying behavior.

Wife:	Occasionally there will be things that I don't purchase because my husband may feel it's too extravagant. I don't feel it's too extravagant but he might.
Interviewer:	Can you give me an example?
Wife:	You're going to laugh! I like (named specialty store) when I am in the mall. I may want to get their antibacterial soap that may cost ten dollars when we could go to (named discount store) and get the equivalent for maybe a dollar. And if he is with me I will not buy things like that. It would just drive him crazy until we left the store or until we got home. That kind of thing definitely stands out, but you know if

> I come back and I'm alone and there is something I want you better
> believe I'll do it. I won't take it home and hide it but it's just easier not
> to have to deal with "I can't believe you're buying that."

At the surface level this quote could be considered an example of buying soap.
At another level, however, it's an example of strategies women use to buy what
they want. And this particular strategy consists of the activities of (a) delaying
the purchase, (b) returning to the mall alone, and (c) buying the product. For
other participants this strategy extended to (d) hiding the purchase at home, and
(e) having it magically appear at a later date. The objects varied across interviews,
but the strategies were very much the same.

Consider the following portion of the same transcript. The wife is talking
about buying clothes.

> Our tastes are different. If I ask him what he thinks, and he agrees, then that's
> good. But if we disagree, then I get what I want anyway.

The exchange is about buying clothes, of course, but at another level of analysis it
could be labeled "preferencing judgment" because the participant gives greater
value to her own judgment than to her husband's. Now we have two strategies
that suggest how women get their way: (a) shopping alone and (b) preferencing
judgment.

In subsequent interviews, we would look for additional examples of these two
strategies and for additional strategies as well. In developing our list of strategies,
it's not necessary that each participant reveal or engage in each one. We're only
trying to identify and understand the use of such strategies, not make a claim
about the distribution of the strategies among the participants.

Knowing that shoppers use such strategies provides insight into developing
a creative theme and constructing the visuals for messages. In our example of
women's shopping strategies, it's likely that the women need confirmation that
they're doing the right thing. Constructing messages that implicitly condone the
shopping strategies revealed in the interviews, that reinforce the correctness of
independent female shopper judgment, and that express the value of self-reward
allow the advertiser to fit the message within the reality constructed by the shopper. Given that the strategies are really little games that wives play with their hus-
bands, a light-hearted tone would also seem to be appropriate.

Qualitative data analysis is nonlinear and sometimes quite messy. Researchers
are great doodlers, writing down concepts, drawing lines of relationship from
one concept to another, listing conditions under which things occur, and mark-
ing up transcripts with questions and observations. It's all part of the job of analysis. Don't be concerned if you can't immediately find all the relationships in

your data. They have a way of hiding from you and then all of a sudden popping out. Gaining insight is a creative process over which the planner does not have total control. It may take a dozen iterations before anything or everything begins to make sense.

Interviewing Groups

Rather than interviewing individuals one at a time, interviewing groups of individuals can be more economical and faster and produce data from participant interaction that would not be available otherwise.

Advertising research has a history of convening groups of individuals in rooms with see-through mirrors and videotaping capabilities and then asking a series of questions related to an advertising problem. This technique—focus groups—has been much abused because it has primarily sought confirmation of researchers' ideas and concepts rather than seeking meaning from the insider's perspective. Most of all, it violates the qualitative tenet of going to the participants and conducting the research in a natural setting.

However, group interviewing may be quite appropriate when (a) we can judge without doubt that the topic of interest is of considerable importance to the participants selected; (b) we want to add to or confirm what we've discovered through other research methods; and (c) the behavior we want to understand occurs naturally in a group setting. Certain events in participants' lives carry great importance. These might include, for example, choosing a college, getting married, having children, getting divorced, suffering a life-threatening disease, or buying a home. Gathering diverse individuals into a single group to discuss these experiences would be more economical than interviewing each person individually. If you're forming a group of consumers based on brand purchase, then it's better to select brand loyalists or heavy users of the product if you want to gather meaningful data that can provide insight into buying patterns. Qualitative interviewing deals with the things of importance in the everyday lives of individuals. But just because something is of great importance to the planner doesn't mean that it's of equal importance to the participants.

New mothers are very concerned about what they feed their babies and such concern may obviously lead to choosing one brand of baby food over another. It is the new motherhood status that binds the group, not reliance on a particular brand, and the insight you seek is the connection between motherhood and brand choice, not just brand usage.

Sometimes a researcher will conduct individual interviews with consumers to develop initial insight and then add in more economical discussion groups consisting of the same or similar people. If the situation warrants it, that's fine, but you need to be aware that the order in which you use research methods can affect the results of your study. Because of the social sensitivity of some behaviors and purchases, it is better to conduct the personal interviews first and follow them with focus groups. A person may express a socially correct opinion in a group and then feel compelled to maintain that opinion during an individual interview as well. If there is doubt about which method to use first, choose individual interviewing before conducting group interviews.

After completing 10 to 12 individual interviews, you may wonder if your initial interpretations of the data are valid. At this point, planners will sometimes ask the individuals who have been interviewed to convene as a group to evaluate the research results. Such a group meeting not only has the advantage of helping with the data analysis but also provides additional data and insight as group members interact with each other.

Sometimes the behavior you primarily want to understand is group behavior. Keeping in mind the importance of contextual meaning in qualitative research, adherence to its theoretical foundation suggests that studying the behavior in the group setting is appropriate. Consider, as an example, "What do school children eat for lunch?" We could ask the parent who prepares the lunch, but the parent could not answer the question. He knows only what is prepared and packed for the child's lunch. We could even do an inventory of lunch bags as children entered the school or the cafeteria at lunch. But this would again tell us only what has been prepared, not what is actually being eaten for lunch. Obviously, sitting at the table in the natural surroundings of the lunchroom, observing and interacting with the children, is more likely to provide a reliable answer. There we might encounter the trading of lunch items that often occurs and observe what children are actually eating.

Families constitute another important form of group behavior. Within a family each individual family member will have a different interpretation about how the family functions and where decision making occurs.

For example, individually interviewing spouses in long-lasting marriages about threats to their marriage over the years will produce some similar interpretations among spouses. Yet for one spouse what was regarded as a tough time was not experienced similarly by the other. When you interview the spouses together, you discover a slightly different shared interpretation of the marriage. Is one more accurate than the other? Of course not. In a qualitative world, there are multiple meanings associated with events and all are equally true. One is not privileged over the other.

If you interview families about certain day-to-day activities, such as renting videotapes for the family to watch, selecting where to dine out, or deciding where to go on vacation, you'll discover individual truths as well as a family truth. The same would be true if you were to interview members of work groups. There are individual interpretations as well as a shared, social interpretation. Whether one is more or less applicable than another depends upon why you're conducting the research. If your aim is to influence family choice of a vacation destination, then you need to understand the family decision-making process (if, in fact, there is one) and the role that each family member plays in it. Is Dad relegated to paying the bills and approving the final choice while Mom and the kids surf the World Wide Web and read brochures to develop the list of places to choose from? Or do Dad or Mom present a list of reasonable choices and other family members choose the final destination? A simple question posed to the family, such as, "Tell me how you decided as a family where you last went on vacation," can produce several extended narratives, with family members correcting and contradicting each other. Whether to do individual or family interviews in this case would depend on your ability to identify the major decision maker, if there is one. Even at that, you might find that other family members exert a powerful influence on the decision maker.

When You Can't Gain Access to the Natural Setting

Interviewing is considered one of the primary data collection methods in qualitative research. Sometimes, however, participants are reluctant to give you access to their homes, families, or work places. In these situations—and sometimes for reason of economy—the planner might be restricted to conducting the interview by telephone or by e-mail correspondence. In such interviews you may lose much contextual information about the person or about decision making.

If you wanted to interview presidents of companies, for example, they might be unwilling to grant you a face-to-face interview of unspecified length. In such cases you can agree to a specified length of, say, 20 minutes, hoping that once the interview is under way, the participant may choose to extend the time. We have seen this occur from time to time because even very busy corporate executives enjoy talking about their lives and work when they have the undivided, interested attention of a planner.

When the participants you want to interview are widely scattered geographically and your research budget is small, you may choose to interview by telephone, recognizing that you will lose contextual information. In such cases, it's best to arrange in advance a time and date for the telephone call. You can proceed much as you would in a face-to-face interview, but know that you'll be totally dependent on sound and tone of voice to help guide you. As you would in other interview situations, you can also easily record the telephone interview and produce a transcription for analysis.

Two other ways to gather interview-like qualitative data are by traditional mail survey and by e-mail. With these techniques much more responsibility and labor are placed upon the participant, and the opportunities for the spontaneous prompt and requests for clarification are almost nil. However, as long as you allow participants to respond to your questions from their own perspectives and in their own words, you should be able to gain insight, though limited, into their worlds of meaning.

Summary

Qualitative interviewing is an intellectually demanding, time-consuming process. Its goal, like all qualitative research, is to come to understand the meaningful world of participants as they understand it themselves.

Conducting good qualitative interviews takes time, patience, and practice; interview skills develop over time.

Qualitative interviews can be conducted with individuals, with groups of individuals, in naturally occurring groups, or in a combination of these. Identifying relationships in qualitative data is a creative process over which the researcher does not have total control.

Qualitative interviews should be conducted in natural settings using an interview guide of no more than four or five topics. Discussion should move from the general to the specific and should always begin at least one level of abstraction above the researcher's topic of interest. Qualitative interviews may last from 30 minutes to 2 hours, depending on interviewer skill and interest level of the participant.

Qualitative interviewing assumes that participants are able to describe the worlds they live in and that they're willing to do so. Some researchers believe that some information may be below the threshold of consciousness, and even if willing, participants are unable to access it directly. Others believe that some information is so sensitive that participants are unwilling to talk about it. In these situations planners may turn to projective techniques to help them understand the participants' worlds of meaning. The following chapter discusses the use of these techniques. Are you a donkey or a lion? Read on.

Key Terms

Coding scheme: A set of categories into which most of what participants say can be assigned

Data sheet: A sheet of paper for recording relevant demographic data about each participant in the study

Emic: From the participant's perspective, using the participant's own words

Etic: From the researcher's perspective, often laden with research jargon that only researchers understand

Group interview: Interviewing several individuals at the same time about the same topic. Group interviews allow for interaction among participants.

Interview guide: A list of four or five topics to be covered in an interview

Natural setting: Any location where the behavior to be studied occurs naturally

Redundancy: A point in interviewing at which no new information is being revealed

Transcript: A written, verbatim record of an interview

Exercises

1. Resonance message strategies present emotions and memories that have counterparts in the experiences of a group of people. For your generation, what would be some typical resonating experiences and emotions? How do these differ from the experiences and emotions of your parents' generation?

2. In 21st-century America it would be considered an insult to give your child the same name as the child of your sister. We're much too individualistic for that. But this has not always been the case. Naming children follows different patterns in different cultures. See if you can gain insight to the naming pattern followed here. William is Henry's older brother. William marries Elizabeth and Henry marries Mary. Henry and Mary name their first male child William. Shortly thereafter, William and Elizabeth have their first child, a male, and name it William.

Then William and Elizabeth have a second son, whom they also name William. Henry and Mary have a second son, whom they name Henry. What is the name of William and Henry's father?

Given this practice you can appreciate the need for nicknames such as "Tall William," "Big William," and "Short William."

3. Here is a partial transcript of an interview with a teenage girl who is describing her clothing purchases. What emic words can you identify?

I needed a new dress to go to New York, so my mother and I went to the mall to look for one. I found this really cool cocktail dress. It was cut low and a bit short, and really phat. My mother said it make me look skanky, so I didn't buy it. But I really wanted that blue dress. Instead I bought a turquoise one. It's okay, but it's not the one I wanted. But I don't want to go around looking like a hootchie mama either.

Related Reading

McCracken, G. (1988). *The long interview.* Newbury Park, CA: Sage.

Miles, M. B., & Huberman, A. M. (1994). *Qualitative data analysis: An expanded sourcebook* (2nd ed.). Thousand Oaks, CA: Sage.

Morgan, D. (1988). *Focus groups as qualitative research.* Newbury Park, CA: Sage.

5

Projective Techniques

What would your response be if you found out that customers for an account you're working on described your client as a donkey but the employees who worked at the company described themselves as racehorses, jaguars, or lions? What kinds of conclusions could you draw from these data? Well, you might reach the same conclusion as NOP Research Group, the market research agency that conducted this study for an office equipment manufacturer. The client ordered this research after suspecting that its customers did not feel the same way about the company as the employees who worked there (NOP Research Group, 2001). To figure out whether the client was correct, NOP conducted in-depth interviews with customers. Included in the interviews was the question, "If this company was an animal, what animal would it be?" Analysis of the data suggested that the company's employees and customers held vastly different perceptions of it, donkeys and lions being quite different, after all. The results of this research helped determine that an image problem existed; steps were subsequently taken by the client to correct the image problem and improve business practices.

It's a simple fact that it is possible to uncover what people think and feel by asking them a direct question in the context of an interview. But that doesn't always work. In the typical interview, participants don't always feel comfortable sharing their innermost feelings with a stranger, and that's often what the researcher is. Furthermore, consumers sometimes just aren't sure why they buy a product or choose one brand over another because the reason is buried deep in their conscious. And even if they do know why they buy, consumers sometimes don't want to appear irrational or stupid. They want to appear normal and will give you socially acceptable answers. Or, they'll avoid telling you exactly what they think just to be polite. In short, a lot of times people—for a variety of reasons—just aren't very straight up with interviewers.

In these instances, the inability to get at a consumer's real feelings can be a problem. Let's use two brands of toilet paper as an example: Charmin (a national brand) and Angel Soft (a regional brand). In some instances, a consumer might choose Angel Soft simply because she likes the picture of an angel on the packaging. To her, angels are soft and gentle and she sees them as keeping watch over her children. In fact, she used angels as part of the decorating motif in her baby's room. But, she thinks that these reasons sound frivolous and aren't exactly good reasons to buy a brand. So, she might tell an interviewer that she purchases Angel Soft over Charmin because it's cheaper/softer/her husband likes it, and so on. All of these would sound like perfectly good reasons to buy a brand, and the interviewer would probably accept them at face value. But they aren't the real reasons why she buys Angel Soft—it's the angels. The influence of the product packaging—the association of angels with the brand—would be important for an interviewer to know, but direct questioning wouldn't uncover it.

Let's take another scenario. Let's say that you were interviewing the same consumer and showed her different characters associated with toilet paper and asked her what each meant: Mr. Whipple, angels, pastel flowers, clouds, horses, puppies—all of those visuals you associate with toilet paper and a couple you don't (just so she wouldn't guess what your real intentions are). Using a visual stimulus, she might be more prone to fess up to the meaning of angels in her life. The visual stimulus might also open the floodgates to information leading to insights about the influence of packaging on her purchase decisions. And the researcher would know that the real reason she buys Angel Soft is because of the angels.

The approach that helped in the above example is called a projective technique. Projective techniques involve the use of stimuli that allow participants to project their subjective or deep-seated beliefs onto other people or objects. According to Donoghue (2000), projective techniques uncover a person's innermost thoughts and feelings and are based on the idea that unconscious desires and feelings can be explored by presenting a participant with an unthreatening situation in which the participant is free to interpret and respond to the stimuli.

Unlike stimuli used in other types of research—for example, you can think of a survey as a type of stimulus in that it triggers respondents to do something such as select an answer from a limited number of options—the stimuli used in projective techniques are less structured and more effective at getting around consumers' built-in censoring devices. This makes them particularly useful for uncovering honest information about topics that might be sensitive or embarrassing. They are also useful for uncovering subtle differences in how consumers feel about products in categories where no obvious differences exist (like our toilet paper example). Because there are no right or wrong answers, researchers hope that participants will project their real feelings in their answers. Deeply personal emotions are usually shared by human beings across the board (Hollander, 1988). So, if planners can tap into these emotions, they might be able to discover the types of insights that lead to successful advertising.

With virtually all projective techniques, the benefit is in the discussion that accompanies the use of the stimulus and not in the stimulus per se. The stimulus itself usually serves mainly to help participants collect their thoughts and explain concepts or ideas (Krueger, 1998). Given this, projective techniques are useful in either one-on-one interviewing or in group settings, and each context has its advantages and disadvantages (Bengston, 1982). Individual interviews can elicit responses that are untainted by group or peer pressure, but they don't capitalize on the dynamic that group thinking allows, the generation of ideas that are raised when one person responds in a way that stimulates the responses of other group members. One-on-one interviews can yield more detailed information, but group interviews are better at uncovering a wider range of ideas. Bengston (1982) also suggests that projective techniques work better in one-on-one interviews due to the ease of administering them and probing responses, as well as their appropriateness for getting at confidential information that a participant might be reluctant to divulge in a group setting.

History of Projective Techniques

According to Rabin (1981), "The penchant of man for imposing his own ideas and interpretations upon unstructured stimuli was noted, and occasionally recorded, centuries ago" (p. 1) and was evident as early as the time of Leonardo da Vinci. However, projective techniques are most often associated with the field of psychology, where their use can be traced back to the mid-1800s. These early attempts lacked a systematic means of analysis, however, and it wasn't until the end of the 19th century that psychologists began using projective techniques in a more rigorous fashion. These early attempts largely concerned the use of inkblots (which came to be known as Rorschach tests), imaginative productions (such as stories told to pictures or other visual cues), and word association tests (which were first used as instruments for detecting guilt in persons suspected of crimes; Rabin, 1981; Semeonoff, 1976). These early efforts did not become known as projective techniques or projective methods until the late 1930s (Rabin, 1981); by the 1960s they were widely embraced by motivational researchers (Robertson & Joselyn, 1974).

Piirto (1990) credits Ernest Dichter, a motivational researcher, with introducing Freudian psychology to market research. According to Kassarjian (1974), projective techniques have been used in marketing research since shortly after World War II. The first published report—and most widely cited study—on market research using projective techniques was a study by Mason Haire, a behavioral scientist, in 1950. Haire assessed consumers' attitudes toward a product innovation—Nescafe instant coffee—by presenting shopping lists to two groups of 50 women. The only difference in the two lists was in the coffee product that each contained; one list included Nescafe and the other included Maxwell House drip coffee. After reviewing the two lists, participants were asked to write a paragraph describing the women to whom each list belonged. The Maxwell House woman was described in more positive terms than the Nescafe woman. The Maxwell House woman was viewed as a "good" housewife, whereas the Nescafe woman was described as "lazy," "sloppy," and not a planner (Fram & Cibotti, 1991). To determine whether the negative attitudes were the result of Nescafe, Haire added a fictitious convenience product and repeated the test. The results from this second round of participants resulted in each woman being viewed unfavorably. Haire attributed the common negative findings to the "prepared-food-character" of the products (Fram & Cibotti, 1991). Next, Haire conducted a third phase of the study. He presented the Nescafe list to 50 women in their homes, again asking them to write a descriptive paragraph. Coupled with this, researchers administering the stimulus asked to look in the participants' pantries to see whether they had purchased Nescafe. They found that those who wrote unfavorably about the Nescafe woman didn't have Nescafe in their pantries. Conversely, those who were more favorable toward the Nescafe woman also tended to use the product (Fram & Cibotti, 1991).

Until relatively recently the use of projective techniques has been sporadic and nonuniform, mainly due to questions of validity and reliability. Nevertheless, projective techniques have become popular in market research. One reason is their cost efficiency—it often costs much less to use projective techniques in the context of interviewing than it does to conduct segmentation studies that might not yield as good information. Most agencies now report that they use projective techniques more frequently and segmentation studies less. However, market parity might also be a reason for the resurgence of these techniques, especially in the advertising industry. According to Piirto (1990), "As consumer spending choices increase, the agency's job of finding the selling hook becomes a search for nuances" (p. 33). Because there's often little that distinguishes competing brands in the eyes of consumers, planners look for small, subtle differences that they might leverage into successful advertising.

Types of Projective Techniques

There are two basic aspects to any projective technique. The first is the stimulus and the second is the participants' response to the stimulus relative to the meaning that the stimulus or situation has for them (Rabin, 1981). Projective techniques have been categorized in terms of the responses required by participants. Donoghue (2000) offers a typology of projective techniques that divides them into five different categories: association, construction, completion, expressive, and choice ordering. This typology is useful for helping explain the differences between the various techniques and, we hope, better illustrates the wide variety of projective techniques available to planners. First, however, a note of caution is in order: A lot of books have been written about projective techniques and can be found in the psychology section of the library or your local bookstore. They'll give you a lot of examples of projective techniques. Just be aware that you can seldom translate these examples directly to the type of research you'll be doing and that you'll need to make adjustments to some established scales in order to answer whatever your question is. Or, you might not find a projective technique that exactly fits what you want to get at, so you might find yourself inventing your own technique (you'll see from the examples below that many ad agencies have done this and have even trademarked their efforts). The thing to keep in mind is that using any projective technique requires skill on the part of the planner. Like conducting interviews, it usually takes using projective techniques a couple of times before you feel comfortable administering them. Also, if your situation requires that you modify or invent your own technique, we strongly urge you to verify the results of your research by triangulating them with other methods until you feel confident that your approach is actually tapping into whatever it is you want to study. We'll talk more about different approaches to triangulation that incorporate projective techniques at the end of this chapter.

ASSOCIATIONS

In association techniques, participants are given a stimulus and are asked to respond with the first words, images, or thoughts that come to mind. The actual response, the speed with which participants answer, and the frequency of a response may all be useful tools for understanding the consumer's relationship with a particular brand or product.

One of the most commonly known and oldest forms of association techniques used in marketing research is word association. Word associations have been used by psychologists since the 1880s and have been linked with marketing since

A group of advertising students working on a class project for Slim Fast's online web site identified the brand's two main competitors as Jenny Craig and Weight Watchers. To get an idea of what women in the target market thought of the three brands, the students conducted a focus group that incorporated a projective technique. The students asked the participants to draw how the three brands would look if each were a person. The drawings were remarkably similar across the participants. Based on the drawings and the questions asked about the meaning behind the pictures, the students concluded that Jenny Craig was the most upscale brand because the pictures the participants drew of the brand reflected nicely dressed and stylish women who were nearing middle age. Similarly, the images that personified Weight Watchers also showed middle-aged women, although they tended to be overweight and not as upscale as the Jenny Craig women. In contrast, the pictures participants drew of Slim Fast showed younger, thin, active women. Coupled with other information gained through the focus group, the students concluded that compared to its main competitors, women in the target market viewed Slim Fast as being for younger and more active women. This insight that was later reflected in the positioning strategy used in the campaign the students developed.

World War II. In word associations, respondents are asked to respond with the first word that comes to mind after reading each word in a list or series of words (Donoghue, 2000; Stevens, Wrenn, Ruddick, & Sherwood, 1997).

To veil your motive and not clue participants in to the actual brand or product being tested, the list often includes "neutral" words—those having nothing to do with the brand (such as carrot, dog, pencil, etc.)—and "key" words that are directly related to the brand (Kassarjian, 1974). In the latter case, think of coffee as an example. Key words for coffee might include *aroma, flavor, Folgers,* and *brown.* If you go back to the toilet paper example we gave you at the beginning of this chapter, you might come up with a list that includes key words like *angel, soft, clouds,* and *white.* A related associative technique is brand personification. This approach requires participants to associate a brand or product with a person or personality type. Participants are given photographs of different people and asked to select those that personify either the brand under consideration or its competitors (or, in some instances, both). If photographs are not available, participants can draw the persons they think personify the different brands.

Word associations can help you elicit a consumer vocabulary or list of words commonly associated with brands or products. This vocabulary list is useful for uncovering a brand's identity or its salient product attributes and may ultimately become part of the creative strategy or the resulting advertisements. Similarly, brand personifications help discover the images that consumers hold of a brand and its competitors. Other uses for word associations and similar techniques include assessing trade name recognition and examining the effects of advertising slogans or promotions (Kassarjian, 1974).

To generate a list of key words for an established brand it is useful to start by looking at past promotional efforts, because these might yield the best trigger words to elicit a response in your participants and help you zero in on key terms. If your goal is to reposition your brand or if your product is new on the market, you might want to start by trying to generate a list of key terms associated with your competitors. Knowing what your brand is (and what it is not) will help determine whether creative strategies should reinforce the brand's image or try to change it.

Association techniques are widely used in advertising. For instance, BBDO Worldwide has actually trademarked their brand personification technique called Photosort (Piirto, 1990). Using this technique, consumers express their feeling about brands by looking at photos of different types of people. Respondents are then asked to make connections between brands and the pictures of people, with the idea that certain types of people personify the users of certain brands and that by making these matches, an account planner can get an idea of a brand's personality. For example, research conducted for General Electric (GE) suggested that consumers thought the brand was conservative and attracted older types. GE subsequently changed this image with the help of its "We Bring Good Things to Life" campaign (Piirto, 1990).

CONSTRUCTION

Construction techniques require participants to construct a story or picture from a stimulus concept. Construction techniques require more complex and controlled intellectual activity than do mere associations because the consumer must take a somewhat abstract association and flesh it out (Donoghue, 2000). Participants in a focus group can be asked to develop and present a collage centered on a topic assigned by the planner. The moderator of the focus group can divide the group in two or three smaller teams, each with at least two people.

Allow about 15 to 30 minutes for participants to prepare their displays. Have materials on hand that will let them add their own words and pictures to the materials you've given them. We've found that access to colored pens or crayons, extra pads of paper, and even things like retail catalogs (don't forget the scissors!) or dictionaries can often help participants better construct a collage about their feelings. After participants have completed the collages, you should have each team present its work and encourage feedback and participation by other members of the group (Krueger, 1998).

A similar constructive technique used by planners involves the use of "bubble" drawings or cartoon tests. Participants are provided with actual visuals or cartoons of people portrayed in situations that are of interest to the planner. Participants are then asked to fill in the bubbles (much like the ones you see in cartoon strips) to indicate what a character is thinking or feeling in the portrayed situation (Donoghue, 2000). These types of exercises are particularly useful when investigating in-store consumer behavior. For example, if you wanted to know how college students decide among various brands of detergent, you could prepare a visual that shows a young college-aged woman standing in the middle of the detergent aisle.

It's important to note that what the planner is most interested in when using construction techniques is the *process* that participants go through in constructing meaning rather than the end result that the process yields. Understandably, these techniques require planners either to question participants continually as they complete the exercise or immediately upon completion of the exercise so that none of the emotion that the participant goes through while making the construction is lost.

Construction techniques work well in both focus groups and one-on-one interviews. However, the complexity of the task that you are asking participants to perform will give you some idea of whether it's appropriate for your specific situation. For example, asking a participant in a one-on-one interview to construct a collage is likely to eat up quite a bit of your interview time. This same task in a group setting, however, is much more manageable and a better use of your time.

COMPLETION

Completion techniques are comparable to word associations in that they tap into similar variables, but they are often considered a bit easier to work with because they better indicate a subject's attitudes and feelings and give good insight into a participant's need-value system (Kassarjian, 1974). With completion techniques, participants are given incomplete sentences, stories, or conversations or are presented with arguments and then asked to complete them. Though this technique can be useful if you have only a limited amount of time with a participant, it requires that you probe participants thoroughly in order to interpret correctly the information that they're giving (Donoghue, 2000).

Kassarjian (1974) notes that most market researchers typically phrase completion questions in either the first person,

> When I think of toilet paper _____

or the third person,

> When people think of toilet paper _____
> The average person who thinks about toilet paper _____

Care should be taken when constructing a completion stimulus because it heavily influences the type of information an interview will generate. When phrased in the third person, completion techniques are highly useful for gaining insight to participants' deep-seated feelings that might be perceived as negative and are therefore hard for a researcher to access. For example, let's say that you are working on behalf of a travel industry client that sells safari packages. You could ask a group of participants whether they might consider Africa as a vacation destination ("I would go to Africa for a vacation because _____"; "I would go to Africa for a vacation if _____"), and, if so, why. We're pretty sure that they'd say something along the lines of "the scenery is breathtaking" or "there are a lot of interesting cultures in Africa." But what do you think they'd say if you asked them why a neighbor might consider Africa for a vacation ("My neighbor would go to Africa for a vacation because _____"; "My neighbor would go to Africa for a vacation if _____")? Chances are you might hear things like "he (or she) likes to show off" or "Africa is where all our friends go on vacation, so they'd go because they've got to go to keep up with the Joneses." These latter two reasons are the real reasons your participants might be considering Africa, and giving them the opportunity to talk about someone else—like their neighbors—enables them to talk freely about attitudes they don't necessarily want to admit they have.

Completion techniques are useful in either one-on-one or group interviewing and are easily administered; generally, the same procedures are followed for both interview types. For example, in a focus group, the planner can pose a sentence to be completed and then give participants a few minutes to complete the task. As a way of promoting discussion, the planner might read the partial sentence and begin asking participants to give their answers and talk about what they were thinking as they completed the task (obviously, you won't have the benefit of the group discussion if you're doing an individual interview). After all participants have had an opportunity to contribute, the planner might ask for their comments, observations, and opinions about what they saw as similar or different in the answers (Krueger, 1998).

EXPRESSIVE

Expressive techniques require participants to role-play, act out, tell a story about, draw, or paint a specific concept or situation (Donoghue, 2000). Role-playing is one expressive technique that works particularly well in situations where participants cannot describe their actions or behaviors in an abstract way, but can demonstrate them (Krueger, 1998). This technique can be used in either individual interviews or in group situations; it is particularly effective in the latter. According to Krueger (1998), in the context of a focus group, "Role playing is helpful in finding out about complex human interactions through demonstrations" (p. 80). In the focus group, the role-playing activity usually occurs with one or two of the members assuming roles and the rest of the group serving as an audience. Krueger notes that the researcher has a dual opportunity to gather data in this type of situation: She can observe firsthand the outcome of the role-playing, and she has the added opportunity for feedback from the rest of the group.

In addition to role-play, other expressive techniques are available for account planners. The most widely used expressive technique in both clinical and marketing research is the thematic apperception test, or TAT (Kassarjian, 1974). When used in marketing research, the TAT is appropriate for such areas as copy-testing (words, visuals, and colors); gaining insight into qualities associated with different products and the people who use them; and exploring attitudes toward products, brands, images of institutions, or symbols. The TAT consists of a series of pictures or cartoons that focus on the research topic but are presented in a situation that is somewhat ambiguous. When using the TAT, participants are asked to assume the role of one of the portrayed people and to construct a story about what the person in the picture is thinking, saying, or doing (Donoghue, 2000). They may also be asked to elaborate on what led to the portrayed scene and what might happen in the future. Themes are developed based on the participants' personal interpretation of the pictures (Zikmund, 1984).

Expressive techniques have been used successfully to discover things about consumers. For example, to find out how teenagers felt about acne for its client Clearasil, D'Arcy Masius Benton & Bowles (DMB&B) used a TAT. After being shown a picture of a person who had a blemish, the teenagers were asked to describe the feelings of the person in the picture. DMB&B found that to teenagers, pimples mean social isolation and being different. As a result, the agency developed a campaign to let teens know that they could get back into life quickly if they used Clearasil. According to a spokesperson for the agency, "We wouldn't have gotten that kind of information if we simply asked them to talk about acne and acne remedies" (Piirto, 1990, p. 33).

As with most other projective techniques, it's imperative to note that the visual must be interesting enough to promote discussion but not so obvious as to give away the purpose of your research. It must also be a visual that's relevant to the participants. By way of illustrating these last two points, Zikmund (1984) relates the story of a research project conducted on why men purchase chain saws. A visual of a man looking at a very large tree was used to explore buying motives among homeowners and weekend woodcutters. The participants' initial reaction to the visual was that it wasn't a job for them but required the help of a professional. In other words, they couldn't relate to the man with the problem, so they didn't consider sawing down the tree themselves as part of the solution. Similarly, when deciding on the stimulus to use in a TAT, the planner should refrain from giving clues that indicate an obvious positive or negative predisposition to any elements of the visual.

The House Where the Brand Lives (or variations thereof) is another common expressive technique used by planners. Planners may introduce a series of brands one by one and then ask the participant to describe the exterior of a house where each of the brands lives. What style of house is it? Is it big? Small? Run down? Well kept? Does it have a porch? How about a yard? What's in the yard? Carrying it a little farther, you can also ask the participants to describe the person who answers the door of the house, others who may live in the house, and what the individual rooms look like. The House Where the Brand Lives offers great insight into a brand's image among consumers and may suggest opportunities in the marketplace.

A beer example offers a good illustration of this. We asked students in an advertising class to describe the houses where two brands of beer—Rolling Rock and Budweiser—live. Although Budweiser has the larger market share, both beers are domestics that are nationally distributed and similarly priced, so they appear to share many similarities. The students described the house where Budweiser "lived" as very middle class and probably located in an older suburb. The house was not large but was well kept. There was a yard with a well-kept lawn. In the yard were toys, suggesting that a family lived there. The man who answered the door was in his thirties, casually dressed, a white-collar worker enjoying a weekend at home. The living room was traditional, containing a sofa, a couple of easy chairs; it was clean but definitely lived-in (toys strewn about, etc.). The living room contained a wide-screen television that was tuned to ESPN where a football game was in progress.

Now contrast this image with the one students constructed for the Rolling Rock home: It was smaller and a bit run-down, possibly in a city. The yard was weedy with a lot of bare spots; in the driveway were a couple of cars, none new (our students called them "beaters"). The home had a porch, on the porch was an old couch. A knock on the door was also answered by a man, but this man had on a T-shirt with a couple of stains; he was a blue-collar worker. The man looked like he may have been woken by the knock on the door. His living room also contained a couch and a couple of chairs, but they were a bit threadbare. From the looks of his home, he lived alone. He had a television but it wasn't wide-screen. The television was tuned to a wrestling match on WTBS.

What conclusions can your draw from the above descriptions concerning the brand images of these two beers? An obvious one is that the image of Budweiser was a bit more upper class than that of Rolling Rock. Looking deeper into the data, you could conclude that Budweiser is a more mainstream beer, very middle class, the beer of choice of a "regular" guy. In contrast, Rolling Rock is a much more blue-collar beer. And that's not necessarily a bad thing considering that Rolling Rock beer has its own niche in the market and does quite well. But, the students' descriptions certainly describe two different images, both of which might certainly influence creative strategy (e.g., these descriptions suggest that it would be hard to position either of these beers as the beverage of choice for the sophisticated man).

CHOICE ORDERING

Donoghue (2000) notes that choice ordering techniques are frequently used in quantitative research but can also be used informally in qualitative research. Techniques of this type require participants to explain why certain things are more important than others. After giving a stimulus that asks participants to rank a list of product benefits from *most important* to *least important,* a planner will use probing questions to find out why participants designated some benefits as more important than others. Choice ordering techniques are also useful when you want participants to rank or order characteristics associated with a product, brand, or service (Donoghue, 2000).

Advantages and Disadvantages of Projective Techniques

The primary disadvantage of using projective techniques is the complexity of the data and the skills required by a planner to analyze the data. This is especially true for those who are not very familiar with qualitative data analysis. Nevertheless, qualitative data analysis is a *learned* skill and one that becomes easier the more often you do it. Because of the complexity of the task, many planners opt to hire out research requiring the use of projective techniques. That leads to another disadvantage: The use of interviewers skilled in administering and analyzing projective techniques is often expensive. However, even if a planner opts to hire out research incorporating these techniques, the planner still needs to understand their utility and have an idea of data analysis in order to evaluate the quality of the outside researcher's work. We discuss different approaches to analyzing data from projective techniques at the end of this chapter; the data analysis techniques we recommend are essentially those that apply to most qualitative research and were discussed earlier in this book.

Donoghue (2000) points out that insights generated by projective techniques are usually not considered representative of a larger population because the samples often aren't large enough to perform tests that have statistical significance. However, the type of insights that planners are looking for begin with consumers themselves, and a single comment by one individual might lead to the insight you're looking for. If necessary, that insight can later be followed up with a larger number of consumers.

The nature of some projective techniques also calls into question the reliability and validity of what is being measured. Reliability refers to the idea that a good research measure yields data that are stable (e.g., the chance that you'll see similar results if you perform the same research with a like group of participants). Validity refers to whether the technique is measuring what it is supposed to measure. In other words, how do you know that the bubble cartoon a participant filled in actually reflects what the participant feels? The issues of reliability and validity associated with projective data have often led to criticism of their use.

Another disadvantage of projective techniques is that it may be difficult to get participants to take part in them. For example, some subjects might refuse or be uncomfortable participating in such things as role-playing exercises. Administering and encouraging participation in these types of research often requires a skilled interviewer.

Despite their limitations, there are many advantages to using projective techniques. The main one is the amount, richness, and accuracy of the information that can be collected (Donoghue, 2000). This is especially true in cases where the focus of study is a person's beliefs, values, motivations, personality, or other unique behaviors (such as product purchases!), which are not easily measured or uncovered using more traditional research methods.

Projective techniques are also useful in the context of a focus group for stimulating discussion or breaking the ice. Participants tend to enjoy projective techniques, and they can inflect new energy into a focus group and lighten the mood of the research (Donoghue, 2000).

Projective techniques are a good way to get truthful responses from participants because participants often aren't sure what you're trying to measure and so don't feel like they are at risk of giving socially unacceptable answers. And, even if they are aware of the general purpose of the research, they often aren't quite sure what aspects of it a planner is interested in. Because the tasks that participants are called upon to do are more free-form and unstructured than traditional research approaches, participants do not perceive their answers to be right or wrong and can be easily encouraged to respond with a wide range of ideas (Donoghue, 2000). Projective techniques also require little in the way of literacy skills, which widens their scope beyond what might be included in a survey or measured via an experiment. This lack of literacy requirements also makes some projective techniques particularly appropriate for children or other populations that are unable or unwilling to articulate their feeling using written words.

Data Analysis

You might think that it's your job to interpret data generated from projective techniques, but it's actually the job of the participants along with your helpful guidance (Krueger, 1998). Nevertheless, ideas rarely come directly from consumers so a planner needs to develop the skills to make connections that will uncover marketplace opportunities.

According to Donoghue (2000) there are two approaches to analyzing projective data. The first is to approach the data quantitatively, whereby the planner classifies the content into categories that are given numerical values. The specific categories can then be tabulated and used to evaluate a subject's responses or the frequency of responses by groups.

For example, let's say you're conducting research on coffee. You might look over the answers participants gave on the projective tests you conducted and group the answers dealing with color or the visual aspects of coffee (dark brown, cream colored, rich looking) into a category titled Appearance. Then, after categorizing all of the participants' answers in this way, you might find that coffee's appearance was cited very often by participants and conclude that appearance is important to consumers. In and of itself, that finding isn't going to be very important unless you know *why*. Although quantitative analysis of the answers may be useful in situations such as uncovering the frequency of certain responses, looking at "top of the mind" characteristics of a product, or trying to plot a conceptual map based on consumer opinions and attitudes, it often doesn't result in the type of insights planners tend to seek. As we mentioned before, it's important to consider the answers participants give in context. You should be aware that using any of the projective techniques we've discussed in this chapter requires a great deal of follow-up questioning and probing on the part of the planner to establish the context of the answer and give it meaning.

As noted in Chapter 2, computers are another option for data analysis and are sometimes useful tools for organizing projective data. Several computer programs on the market, including NUD*IST and ETHNOGRAPH, are widely embraced by researchers looking for a systematic way of analyzing qualitative data. Other agencies use proprietary programs developed in-house. In fact, several agencies have actually trademarked computer programs that were developed for data analysis. For example, the Leo Burnett advertising agency has developed what it calls the Emotional Lexicon, "an interactive computerized system that studies emotions derived from product categories" (Piirto, 1990, p. 35). This computerized system leads a participant through an interview containing certain key words or phrases developed to represent a number of different emotional dimensions that can be reduced to 15 key points. According to a Leo Burnett spokesperson, these data enable the agency to pinpoint whether consumers develop product preferences based on emotional or rational choices.

The second approach to projective data is qualitative analysis. Qualitative analysis and interpretation of projective data are really no different from how qualitative data are usually analyzed. As opposed to categorizing the data by numbers, qualitative data analysis is much more focused on trying to uncover patterns in the data that give insight to what lies behind or is meant by the projections. Krueger (1998) recommends a two-part strategy that involves both participant assistance and multiple data sources to analyze the data gathered from projective techniques. He recommends that you begin by asking participants exactly what their answers mean and what part of an answer you should focus on. In other words, what's the important part of what they're really saying? As you ask this question of more and more participants (either over the course of several focus groups or as you continue conducting interviews), you should begin to see patterns of responses emerge. As these patterns solidify, you'll gain confidence that the answers you're seeing are actually the way that the target market feels about whatever issue you're looking at.

The second part of Krueger's recommended strategy deals with trying to see if you can get the same patterns of data to emerge using more than one method. He notes that projective techniques are but one aspect of reality and they should be checked against other ways of getting at the answer to the questions you're asking. In academe, we call this approach triangulation, which is rather a fancy way of saying that different methods looking at the same problem and asking the same questions should yield similar results. So, you might use a combination of projective techniques to see if you arrive at similar answers, or you might try another combination of methods. This can often be done with the same group of participants in the same session.

For example, a study conducted by Market Research Organization for Commercial Market Strategies (CMS) sought to explore women's attitudes about different forms of contraception (NOP Research Group, 2001; Commercial Market Strategies, 2001). To do so, CMS conducted research among three groups of women of reproductive age who were selected based on demographic characteristics and familiarity with a range of contraceptive methods. Each participant was interviewed individually and asked to read a brief medical record about a fictitious young woman with three children. There was only one difference in the account that the women in each group read: the woman's method of contraception. The women in one group were told that the woman had had a surgical procedure performed to prevent contraception, women in the second group were told that she used the rhythm method, and women in the last group read that she used an IUD. After reading the account, the women were asked to talk about the woman in the medical record: What kind of family life did she have? What kind of wife and mother was she? Did the participants see her as risky or conservative? Was she modern or traditional? The participants were also asked to indicate how much they agreed or disagreed with a similar set of statements about the woman in the record.

After these data were analyzed, the results indicated that the three groups had very different impressions of the fictitious woman. Because the only thing that varied in the accounts the three groups read was the method of contraception, their answers offered interesting insights into how they viewed the three forms of contraception. The participants viewed the woman who had the surgical procedure negatively: She was seen as uneducated, in poor health, living in poverty and largely indifferent to the needs of her family. The group who read that the woman used the rhythm method for contraception viewed her as old fashioned and unreliable, decent but out of the mainstream. She was also seen as a risk taker because her contraception method was unreliable. The woman who used the IUD, in contrast, was well regarded by the women who read her story. She was viewed as modern and a good mother and wife. She was also considered stable, well educated, and conservative (because her contraceptive method had been around a while and was trusted).

This example serves to drive home the importance of triangulation. Three different ways of getting respondents to answer the question were used: traditional one-on-one interviewing and two projective techniques (expression and choice ordering). Separately, they all suggested the same thing about the participants' views about contraception. But taken together, the different approaches reinforced the patterns the researchers were seeing and also helped flesh out the answers better than if only one method had been used. As with all data analysis, the key is to try to see whether the patterns that emerge are valid—that is, are they really answering what you're trying to answer—and similar despite the different approaches. It's kind of like not putting all your eggs in one basket.

Summary

Projective techniques involve the use of stimuli that allow participants to project their subjective or deep-seated beliefs onto other people or objects. The general idea behind these techniques is that a researcher can explore unconscious desires and feelings by presenting participants with unthreatening situations to which they interpret and respond.

Projective techniques are extremely useful for uncovering honest information about topics that might be sensitive or embarrassing or for uncovering subtle differences in how consumers feel about products in categories where no obvious differences exist.

There are two basic aspects to any projective technique: the stimulus and the response to the stimulus. Projective techniques can be grouped into categories such as association, construction, completion, expressive, and choice ordering.

Projective techniques are used in the process of interviewing and are usually appropriate for either one-on-one or group interviews.

There are advantages and disadvantages to using projective techniques. The main advantages are the amount, richness, and accuracy of the information that can be collected, its usefulness for stimulating discussion, and its ability to elicit responses to sensitive questions. The main disadvantages are the complexity of the data and the high level of skill required by a planner to analyze the data as well as questions about the reliability and validity of data that the techniques yield.

At this point, you're probably getting a better idea of why planners are often called creative researchers. In the next chapter, we shift our focus to another innovative way to gather information about consumers—online! If you think that conducting interviews and focus groups through the Internet or e-mail can help you tap into consumer insights, then we've got some great ideas you can use. Read on.

Key Terms

Association: Projective technique in which participants are given a stimulus and are then asked to respond with the first words, images, or thoughts that come to mind.

Choice ordering: Projective technique that requires participants to explain why certain things are more important than others. Participants are given a stimulus and then asked to rank order a list of associated benefits or features from *most important* to *least important*.

Completion: Projective technique in which participants are given incomplete sentences, stories, or conversations or are presented with arguments and then asked to complete them.

Construction: Projective technique that requires participants to construct a story or picture from a stimulus concept. Construction techniques require more complex and controlled intellectual activity than do mere associations.

Expressive: Projective technique in which participants are required to role-play, act out, tell a story about, draw, or paint a specific concept or situation.

Projective techniques: Psychological approaches involving the use of stimuli that allow participants to project their subjective or deep-seated beliefs onto other people or objects. The general idea behind these techniques is that unconscious desires and feelings can be explored by presenting a participant with a stimulus in an unthreatening situation so the participant is free to interpret and respond to the stimulus.

Stimulus: Object used in projective techniques to which the participant responds. Common stimuli for advertising research include collages, brand names, trademarks, slogans, and commercials.

Exercises

1. Select a product category that has several well-known competitors. Form a group of three or four of your classmates or peers. Ask the members of the group to draw a picture of a person to personify each brand. Make sure they do this individually. Tell them to draw as well as they can, but stress that artistic skills don't matter. When finished, tape the pictures grouped by brand to a wall where all members can see them. Examine the pictures and attempt to identify commonalities between the pictures in each group and differences across groups. Based on your findings, write a description of the person that typifies each brand.

2. Go to your local grocery store and take a picture of a group of products in the same product category (e.g., if you are interested in cereal, take the picture in the cereal aisle). Make sure to get several different brands in your shot. Then, on a piece of white paper, sketch the back of a person with a cartoon bubble coming from the top of her head. Try to make the person fairly "formless" and without too many identifying characteristics. Paste the person on top of the photo. Make copies and ask several different people to fill in the bubble and tell you what the person in the picture is thinking about. You can carry this one step farther by asking your participants to create a story about the scenario: What led the person to be in the cereal aisle? On what basis will she make her decision? Is she buying the cereal for herself or someone else? What will happen after she takes the cereal home? Make sure you probe the participants about their responses.

Related Reading

Fortini-Campbell, L. (2001). *Hitting the sweet spot.* Chicago: Copy Workshop.

Rabin, A. I. (1981). *Assessment with projective techniques. A concise introduction.* New York: Springer.

Rotenberg, R. H. (1995). *A manager's guide to marketing research.* Toronto: Dryden.

Zikmund, W. G. (1997). *Exploring marketing research* (6th ed.). Orlando, FL: Dryden.

6

Qualitative Research Online

Focus Groups and Interviews

What do the U.S. Department of Defense (DOD), a Swiss research institution, the University of Illinois, and the telephone company have in common? They were all important contributors to the phenomenon we know today as the Internet. It's somewhat surprising that a network developed for military-funded research is now one of the most important communication tools in our society. However, a review of the history of the Internet suggests that enhanced communication was always at the core of its development. The U.S. DOD built ARPANET, the precursor to the Internet, in 1969 as a way to link together distinct groups such as universities and research contractors. The DOD also ensured that the physical portions of the network are dispersed throughout the world and are built to withstand multiple nuclear attacks (Goldring, 1997). Telecommunication providers support this infrastructure and provide multiple paths of access that allow for rapid transfer of information. The National Science Foundation took over responsibility for the Internet in the 1980s and promoted it as a way for all manner of researchers and academics to collaborate and share information.

Hand in hand with this institutional development were developments that enhanced opportunities for individuals like us to be part of this networked society. The development and dissemination of the personal computer in the 1980s increased consumer potential to access networked environments. The introduction of the Apple Macintosh created the term *user-friendly,* and many individuals with no previous experience with computers began to accept them into their homes (PBS, 2000).

The National Science Foundation relinquished control over a major part of the Internet in 1993 and sanctioned its use for commercial purposes. The World Wide Web, originally developed at the Swiss research lab CERN, blossomed and grew with the new range of commercial possibilities. Today, this communication power is harnessed by advertising agencies not only to advertise products and services, but also to research and communicate with consumers.

As we write this book, about half of all Americans have access to the Internet. Worldwide, more than 400 million people have Internet access, with these numbers consistently increasing every day. People use the Internet for many reasons: to communicate with friends and family, to find information, to shop, to play games, and to download and listen to music. In fact, about one sixth of the total time an individual spends with electronic media (including the Internet, TV, and radio) is spent online (Rainie & Packel, 2001). Internet access is available not only through computers, but also through televisions, mobile phones, and hand-held devices. Given this usage and availability, it's not surprising that many account planners are looking to the Internet as a new way to collect consumer information.

To date, account planners have implemented both quantitative and qualitative research online. For example, account planners have conducted quantitative surveys online using both e-mail and Web-based data collection methods, with varying degrees of success. One attractive feature of the Internet is the potential for obtaining a large number of responses quickly. For numerous reasons, however, account planners have difficulty determining the generalizability of such surveys. These include the possibility that a single individual can provide multiple responses to a single survey and that responses can be collected from individuals not in the target audience (e.g., children under the age of 18 could respond to online surveys focused on adult products). There isn't any single source, like the U.S. census, that can accurately provide a good picture of the actual demographic makeup of the Internet population, either in the United States or worldwide (Mann & Stewart, 2000). Without such a source, the ability to generate a random sample, so important in quantitative research, is diminished.

Implementing qualitative research programs online is becoming popular among consumer researchers. As with quantitative research, data can be collected quickly from individuals all over the world. Moreover, the generalizability issues associated with quantitative research are not as germane to qualitative research. Two specific types of qualitative research, focus groups and depth interviews, are seen as particularly fitting for the Internet environment. In this chapter, we focus on the use of focus groups and depth interviews online. We describe the types of focus groups and depth interviews that can be conducted online and discuss the pros and cons of each. We also provide guidelines on how best to implement these techniques.

Online Focus Groups

When you think about a traditional focus group, you probably have a picture in your mind of a group of people of the same gender and roughly the same age, sitting around a table with soft drinks, sharing their opinions on a specific topic, product, or service. Take away the table, the soft drinks, and the ability for members of the group to look at one another, and you have an online focus group. What remains is the ability for diverse opinions to be heard.

THE POTENTIAL OF ONLINE FOCUS GROUPS

Harold Bragen, president of ARC Research in Cranford, New Jersey, believes that online focus groups "may constitute the most useful new research technique to appear since the introduction of CATI (computer-assisted telephone interviewing)" (Bragen, 2000, p. 8). Although online focus groups may not be the best choice for all types of advertising and marketing planning research, the technology has many diverse applications. For example, online focus groups can be used to study the following:

- New product concepts in the early stage of development, specifically if category users tend to be heavy users of the Internet. For example, new product concepts could be tested online for marketers of energy drinks or portable mp3 players. Both of these products appeal to young, affluent individuals, a group that spends significant amounts of time online.
- High-level decision makers with busy schedules. Online focus groups can study how these executives make decisions or use products; such executives are unlikely to travel to a facility to participate in a group, yet may be willing to logon to the Web for an hour or two to interact with others in their peer group.
- Marketing opportunities among college students. This demographic group consists of heavy Internet users who often have free access to the Internet. Understanding what motivates such users to purchase various products or services in both the online and offline environments could be studied.
- Banner advertisements and other online advertising offerings. In fact, every type of Web-related topic is a natural for online focus groups.
- Print advertisements and other offline advertising offerings (Bragen, 2000). Online audiences can quickly assess creative work, particularly in the development stage.

Obviously, there are certain types of consumer research that won't be feasible online, such as tests comparing taste preferences (e.g., the famous Pepsi Challenge) and tests of a tactile nature (e.g., comparing one type of fabric or paper to another). Furthermore, if you know that people in your target group are not

Web savvy, then the technical nature of online focus groups would probably be a barrier difficult to overcome.

Many believe that online focus groups will never replace face-to-face focus groups because the "two are different animals" (Greenbaum, 2000). Many research firms see online groups as a complement, not a replacement, to traditional panels. Today, well-known companies such as Burke Research conduct about 10% of their groups online.

STRENGTHS OF ONLINE FOCUS GROUPS

Online focus groups offer several benefits over traditional focus groups. One of the biggest benefits is that there are no geographic barriers to participation: People in the group can come from across the country or around the world. In addition, these participants won't have to pay to travel to a focus group facility or incur other costs (such as child care costs) in order to participate in the group. These factors create a huge pool of potential participants to select from for your focus group. In fact, account planners report that there are many people who won't travel to a facility but who may participate in an online group, and they are often higher-income persons who rarely participate in traditional focus groups.

Online focus groups may be more efficient for account planners, too, in terms of costs and time commitments. One of the biggest cost savings comes from savings in facility costs: Because participants do not travel to a facility for the sessions, you don't have to pay the rental costs for the facility or the travel costs for agency personnel to travel to the facility. Though you may incur some costs for physically setting up the focus group online, these costs are likely to be below those of the facility. You will save time because you can schedule the online focus groups at your or your client's convenience and do not have to worry about scheduling conflicts at the facility. Costs vary for both traditional and online focus groups. One report found that traditional groups can cost up to $100,000 and take months to produce results, whereas online focus groups can be done in a few weeks for as little as $3,500 per group (Wellner, 2000). Transcripts will also be available quickly since participants are typing in their dialogue and creating a transcript as the group progresses. Because online groups can be implemented quickly, you have the opportunity to quickly pinpoint consumer trends and/or reactions to current events.

It is also possible that the responses you would get from online focus groups will be superior to the responses you would get in traditional focus groups. For example, peer pressure online is minimized, because participants are participating in discussions from the privacy of their own environments. Participants cannot judge one another based on appearance, and a single participant will find it difficult to dominate the conversation, even if he or she is an incredibly fast typist! Not being able to see a panel or hear how they talk minimizes the amount of prejudging of the individuals that occurs (Weissman, 1998). Because each participant's voice can be "heard," everyone has an equal voice (Weissman, 1998).

In most cases, because the individual is participating out of his or her home, the participant may experience a greater sense of privacy in an online group than in a traditional group. Without the physical presence of other participants or even a moderator, participants are anonymous and so may be willing to divulge information that they might not divulge in a traditional focus group situation.

UNIQUE CHALLENGES TO ONLINE FOCUS GROUPS

Account planners have identified some challenges to working with online focus groups. These include challenges in participant identification and recruitment, moderator interaction, group process, and content richness.

Participant Identification and Recruitment.   In both traditional and online focus groups, participants are likely to be screened for certain demographic and/or psychographic characteristics before the group actually takes place. If you were recruiting for a focus group on fashion-forward young working women, for example, you might ask about the participant's age, ethnic background, and the types of clothing she purchases. In a traditional focus group, it will be evident if the answers participants gave during the prescreening were true when each participant arrives at the facility (i.e., you would be able to tell that they are women, what their ethnic backgrounds are, their approximate age, etc.). Anyone who does not meet the requirements can be excluded from the group at that time. However, such visual confirmation is not available online. In fact, it would be possible to recruit for a group of fashion-forward young working women and have an online group made up of 80-year-old men! Later in this chapter, we review the different ways to recruit for online focus groups and provide recommendations on how best to screen to make sure that who you want is who you get. Keep in mind, though, that there will always be people who misrepresent themselves online. That's a risk we take as online researchers.

Moderator Interaction and the Group Process.   One of the hallmarks of traditional focus groups is the presence of a moderator who controls the flow of the discussion. Many critics worry that moderators of online focus groups won't be able to establish authority and keep the group on track (Weissman, 1998). The key to addressing this concern is recognizing that online moderators need a set of skills applicable to the online environment in addition to the traditional group moderating skills. For example, moderators in both traditional and online groups need to determine the right amount of time to devote to each question. In a traditional group, the moderator can orally direct the discussion to the next topic. In an online group, however, the moderator can try to close a discussion and type a question that moves the group onto a new topic, but could be ignored by the group. The group could continue to discuss the original topic ad infinitum, much to the distress of the moderator. In a similar vein, the moderator must find ways to control any participants who are damaging the group process. Finally, the moderator must make sure that participants stay for the whole session in order to create the best group dynamic. These specific problems are discussed in a later section on the role of the moderator.

Information Richness.   Arguably, the greatest difference between traditional and online focus groups is the lack of nonverbal cues in the online version. In a traditional group, much can be read into the rolling of eyes, sarcastic tones of voice, nodding heads, and other nonverbal cues that accompany the discussion. The lack of nonverbal cues online, some argue, limits the comprehension that can be obtained from the discussion. Others see the lack of nonverbal cues as a benefit, because an outspoken person may become the focus of the analysis or the discussion in a traditional group interview. As previously mentioned, an online focus group can allow for soft-spoken and quiet people to have the same voice as the others in the group.

In actuality, the lack of nonverbal cues suggests that traditional forms of participant analysis have to be revised when looking at online focus groups. Bragen (2000) suggests that account planners analyzing focus group data use techniques such as close textual analysis or language choice analysis to determine the tone or emotional content of a piece of writing. Therefore, the analysis techniques described earlier in this book can apply to online focus groups.

The Type of Group: Closed-Ended or Open-Ended.   There are two general types of focus groups that account planners choose to analyze online: closed-ended and open-ended. Closed-ended groups attempt to replicate a traditional focus group as closely as possible: Small groups of people are brought together to answer questions posed by a moderator in a special Internet chat room. Like regular focus groups, these sessions last about 90 minutes, and participants are paid for their participation.

Open-ended focus groups occur in a bulletin board or discussion forum environment. An unlimited number of participants can respond to questions posed at a special section of a Web page. Participants can respond to the comments posted by others and may even post questions and topics of their own. As evidenced by its name, an open-ended focus group can go on indefinitely, although you may wish to limit the amount of time specific questions are posted in order to encourage responses to the current question. In addition, communicating that topics change frequently can encourage repeat visits and continual input from discussion forum visitors.

Implementing Online Focus Groups

The up-front planning for an online focus group is identical to the planning for a traditional focus group. Agency and client representatives should meet to discuss exactly what the focus group will be used for. What specifically needs to be learned, and what is the best way to do so? From that meeting, it is possible for the account planner to develop a list of questions that can be used by either the moderators of the closed-ended focus group or posted at a Web site for an open-ended group. It is at this point that some unique implementation requirements and agency/client decisions come into play. These requirements and decisions are unique for the two different types of groups, so the following section treats the two groups separately.

THE CLOSED-ENDED GROUP

In a closed-ended group, a traditional focus group is replicated as closely as possible. A small group of individuals gathers at a designated site at a designated time to discuss a specific topic under the guidance of a moderator. The individuals in the group can be from all over the world, and the designated site is not a traditional focus group facility but an online chat room type of environment. In addition, there are some unique requirements to the online group.

Preplanning. The initial decisions for a closed-ended group are similar to those for a traditional group: decide beforehand the number of groups, when the groups will run, and the question list. When planning the date of the focus group, keep in mind that potential participants will have many other choices of activities in addition to the focus group for which you are recruiting them. Because many of your participants will be participating from home, think in particular about distractions in the home that might interfere with their participation. Schedule your focus group to avoid big television events such as the Super Bowl and season finales of television shows. Studies have shown that the best days to maximize participation are Monday, Tuesday, and Wednesday ("Securing Attendance to Focus Groups," 2000).

Recruitment. There are numerous ways to recruit for online focus groups: online banner ads, links at Web sites, and notices in e-mails, as well as traditional ways like the telephone (Collins, 2000). Services like DoubleClick provide network advertising possibilities in the form of banner advertisements for online advertisers.[1] This means that you would create a banner ad soliciting participation in the online focus group and provide DoubleClick with a description of the type of person you wish to recruit (from a demographic perspective). The banners would then be rotated across the thousands of Web pages that are part of the DoubleClick Network and meet your demographic requirements. Potential participants would click on the banner ad and complete an application form signaling their desire to participate in the group. The application form serves as a screening tool to identify the best possible participants for the focus group: Specific questions on product usage and attitudes should be provided on the form. The selected participants would then be asked to confirm these answers before the start of the group as a way to make sure that the person who replied is the person who is attending the group.

Once the applications are received, the account planner can review the applicants and select a group of between 30 and 40 individuals to be invited to the focus group. With this type of recruitment method, it is possible to receive thousands of completed application forms, many of which may be bogus. Sorting through the thousands of replies takes a large amount of time. Invitations including the date and time of the group can be sent by e-mail, and applicants can respond as to whether they will attend or not. Individuals recruited in this method generally have low "show-up" rates: A study of show-up rates by the trade publication *PR News* ("Securing Attendance to Focus Groups," 2000) recommended that 20 confirmations of attendance are needed to generate a group of 10 individuals.

Other recruitment methods appear to be better techniques for finding possible participants for the focus group. For example, telephone recruitment has been found to obtain a better commitment and participation rate than other methods ("Securing Attendance to Focus Groups," 2000). As with traditional groups, a list of possible participants could be purchased from a supplier with whom you have an already-established relationship. Individuals can be contacted to assess whether they would be both appropriate for and interested in participating in the specific group. In addition, the recruiter should assess whether the individuals have the technical skills (i.e., ability to access the Internet) and resources necessary (e.g., a home computer with modem) to participate in the online group. Because it is likely that many of the individuals contacted may be unfamiliar with the concept of an online focus group, the recruiter contacting the prospects can explain how the online focus group works and answer any questions individuals may have about the process. It is possible that bonding between recruiter and participant helps to increase the chances that the individual recruited will actually show up for the focus group. A *PR News* study

("Securing Attendance to Focus Groups," 2000) indicated that participants pre-screened by telephone have the highest show-up rate (90%).

Another possible recruitment channel would be to recruit through lists of the client company's own consumers. These lists may be obtained through the company's paper records or through e-mail registration at the company's Web site. Persons who are currently involved with a company's products or services may feel a greater commitment to participate; their show-up rates, according to PR News, are about 70%. Of course, the limitation to this type of group is that nonusers and perhaps users of competitive products will not be included in the group.

It is also possible to purchase lists of targeted e-mail addresses of individuals that match your demographic requirements.[2] This procedure is similar to purchasing lists of individuals' telephone numbers. There are several cautions with this method. First, many of these e-mail lists are collected in ways that may violate some consumers' perceptions of privacy. For example, list brokers may collect names and e-mail addresses of individuals who participate in news groups or who post their e-mail address on their Web sites. In these cases, individuals receiving unsolicited e-mail to participate in online focus groups may consider the e-mail to be "spam" and may not appreciate receiving it from you. Therefore, it is important to find a list where the individuals on the list "opted in" to be on the list, that is, they gave their permission. Once such a list is found, it is important to know that the show-up rate for persons on these lists is fairly low: only about 50% ("Securing Attendance to Focus Groups," 2000).

In addition to collecting information about participants, a written application should also provide information to the participants, such as describing what an online chat room format is like for those who have not participated in a similar online activity. The skill level expected of participants should be provided so individuals can determine if they have the keyboarding skills to participate (e.g., do you want participants who can touch type or will hunt-and-peck do?). Also, let participants know that you are looking for ideas, thoughts, and opinions—not spelling and grammar skills.

Given the proliferation of chat rooms online, you may be tempted to forgo any type of recruiting and visit an already existing chat room to conduct your research. For example, a recent television show on PBS showed researchers visiting teen chat rooms and, posing as teens, asking opinions about products and services. To us, this is a violation of research ethics because the researcher is pretending to be someone he is not in order to collect information. In addition, the individuals providing the information have not given their informed consent and are unaware that they are participating in a research project.[3] Finally, remember that New Yorker cartoon: "On the Internet, no one knows you're a dog" (Steiner, 1993, p. 5). If you're pretending to be a teen in a chat room to conduct research, how do you know the others in the chat room aren't bored 30-year-olds?

Software.   Once individuals have been recruited for the group, they need to know where to show up for the session. Most agencies have computers and servers with Internet access; with this technology in place, it is fairly easy to set up a chat room for online focus groups.[4] The expense associated with setting up such a chat room can range from virtually no cost to thousands of dollars for software with proprietary access. Depending on the number and frequency of the groups that you will be conducting, the proprietary software purchase may be a good option. If you will be providing graphics, photographs, music, and video clips for the group to view during the session, be sure to factor that into your server needs and make sure that participants have appropriate software to view the materials. In addition, proprietary software will allow for a chat room with password access. Password access will keep outsiders from entering the group.

You should definitely consult with the Information Technology (IT) experts at your agency about the best software for your agency system and involve them in the process. In fact, it would probably be a good idea to include an IT person in the actual session to address any technical problems or questions in real time. When planning an online focus group, plan for worst-case scenarios with your IT person. What if the server goes down during the session? What if traffic is heavy and it takes a long time for responses to come back? Think through all potential technical problems with your IT person in advance and you'll be free during the session to concentrate on the important information: the interaction with consumers.

Screening and Initial Directions.   During the initial screening, collect specific information from each participant that can be cross-checked immediately before the start of the focus group. For example, participants can be asked for the name of a preferred brand of a product as part of the screening process, and then could be asked this same question again before admittance into the focus group. This serves as one check that the people attending the group are actually the persons who were screened for participation (Maddox, 1998).

Once individuals have been screened, a series of communications should be instigated between the account planner and the participants to keep them enthusiastic about participating in the group. First, a confirmatory e-mail should be sent to participants, asking them to visit the site before the group session to make sure that the site functions with their browsers. Most chat features work adequately with both Internet Explorer and Netscape Navigator. However, some participants might use other browsers and may have trouble accessing the site. It is better to know this in advance of the session so the individual can either choose not to participate or can download a different browser to use during the session.

Once the participants let the account planner know they can access the site, the account planner can send an e-mail reiterating the instructions for the actual group session. A reminder e-mail and/or telephone call the day of the group session is also advisable to make sure participants will show up at the correct time. Keep in mind that participants may be coming from different time zones and be sure to tailor your instructions to the specific time zone of each participant.

The Actual Session. When the day of the session arrives, keep your fingers crossed that your equipment and the network stay up and running during the group. Log on about half an hour before the start of the session to make sure everything is working properly and to greet the participants as they arrive. Some programs allow for an online waiting room separate from the actual focus group. Having an online waiting room or a place for people to gather before the actual discussion allows the group to interact even before the session starts. A designated greeter should check credentials and have a way to confirm that the participant is the person who was invited. The greeter could be the moderator, but having a different greeter (even if in name only) will better replicate the offline experience. If an online waiting room is not available, individuals should be greeted as they log on and be told that the session has not yet begun and that other individuals are waiting for the entire group to gather.

At the designated time, either the moderator should announce that the group is now formally in session, or the group in the waiting room should be requested to log on to the focus group room, which should become activated at the appropriate time. The moderator then becomes in control of the proceedings. The moderator should introduce the participants, encourage them to answer any and all questions posed, and let the participants know that they shouldn't be concerned about spelling and grammar. The moderator can then officially start the focus group.

The qualifications for an online moderator are somewhat similar to those for an offline moderator. The moderator must be a good listener and be able to keep track of all members of the group and encourage their participation. In addition, the moderator should be able to type proficiently, or else have standard questions that can quickly be cut and pasted into dialogue boxes.

Many account planners who have used online focus groups recommend having two moderators. The first moderator's (Moderator A's) role is the same as the moderator in a traditional focus group. Moderator A runs the group and is the only moderator interacting with the group. Moderator A is responsible for setting the tone of the group, introducing the participants, and leading the discussion. However, he or she must be more active in his or her listening than the traditional moderator. Online listening needs to be expressed in words, not silence, as in an offline conversation. Listening with interest means that Moderator A should respond promptly to questions that the participants ask, express interest in particular points made, and ask follow-up questions that refer directly to the information being presented.

The second moderator, Moderator B, interacts with the client from these observers and agency personnel observing the group and reads any incoming messages so he or she can advise Moderator A on follow-up questions as well as client or agency concerns. The two moderators would ideally be sitting side by side so they can communicate verbally with each other; if this is not possible, talking via speaker telephone would be possible. Moderator B should be alert to changes in the tone of the conversation that might signal that a question was misunderstood or suggest that participants would be happy to talk more about something when asked (Mann & Stewart, 2000). Moderator B should also tell Moderator A which participant wants to provide more information. Moderator A is responsible for handling probes and should be sure to name the participant to whom the probe is directed, otherwise, all members of the group may jump in to answer the question posed in the probe.

Certainly, any of the problems or issues that arise in traditional focus groups can also arise in an online group. However, some different techniques may be necessary to deal with such problems. For example, it is possible that one individual will be the dominant individual in the group: He or she may type the same point repeatedly. Moderator A should confirm that the individual is being heard using active listening techniques (e.g., the moderator could type in, "Good point, Susan. What do others think about that?"). If the dominating individual is taking the discussion off topic, the moderator should keep repeating the question until it is answered, perhaps naming the individual who will not get off the topic ("Nancy, those are good points about the product's quality. Let's move on to talk about taste and texture, and if we have time we'll come back to quality at the end of the session."). Don't worry about interrupting the dominating individual as he or she is typing: Interruptions are more acceptable online than face-to-face.

If the moderator feels that she is losing control of the group due to a single individual, remember technology is your friend: You can always instruct your IT professional to cut the individual out of the discussion (now, aren't you glad you asked the IT person to help out during the session?). Although this is certainly the worst case scenario and should only be used in extreme situations, moderators should remember that this option does indeed exist.

After the Session.   At the end of the session, thank the participants and let them know when they can expect to be paid. You may wish to consider an online payment system (such as PayPal) that can transfer funds directly to users' accounts. If checks will be mailed, you should promise to notify the individuals via e-mail when the checks are issued.

One of the good things about an online focus group is that the transcript is immediately available for the moderator's review. The report written by the moderator of an online focus group should follow the same guidelines as one written for an offline focus group.

OPEN-ENDED GROUPS

An open-ended group is a somewhat different type of focus group. The open-ended group uses a bulletin board or discussion forum type of environment to solicit opinions from visitors to Web sites. Basically, a discussion forum is set up at a company or agency Web site, and a link on the home page directs visitors to the discussion forum so they can share their opinions on specific topics. The open-ended group shares some similarities with both surveys and closed-ended groups. As with a survey, it's possible to garner responses from a wide range of people; however, it is difficult to control for demographics because discussion forums tend to be open to all visitors to a Web site, and posters can be anonymous. Also like surveys, responses (known in an open-ended group as postings) are asynchronous, with individuals providing messages and responses to questions to the discussion forum whenever it is convenient to them: Not everyone who is part of the group is online at the same time.

Open-ended groups are similar to closed-ended groups in that participants can react and interact with messages posted by others in the group. Visitors to the Web site discussion forum can reply not only to the question posted by the moderator but also to comments from others visiting the discussion forum. Often, the participants in the discussion forum form a community of like-minded individuals who share ideas and opinions on all manner of topics, not just the topic of interest to account planners. These online communities are seen as a particular and unique strength of the Internet.

Open-ended groups are unique in that topics either can be posted indefinitely, allowing for a range of opinions to be generated, or can be posted for a limited period of time. Therefore, open-ended groups cannot be used in instances where information must be collected in a short period of time. New questions can be added frequently, and the direction of the discussion can evolve based on not only what the account planner wishes to discuss, but also what the participants in the discussion wish to discuss. In some respects, an open-ended group creates a space where visitors can help to shape their own community with the assistance of the moderator. Open-ended groups create ongoing dialogues with participants that can provide a rich text of information about perceptions of brands, advertising, and consumerism.

Preplanning.   The planning for an open-ended group is somewhat different from that for a closed-ended group because the discussion forum is posted for long periods of time and, because a moderator is not constantly present, could take on a life of its own. Therefore, specific decisions and rules should be discussed among agency and client personnel before establishing the forum.

Overall Purpose.   First, the overall purpose of the discussion forum should be decided. Will the discussion forum be a place where any and all discussions about the brand can occur, or will it be focused on a specific topic? For example, Procter & Gamble (P&G) has several different types of discussion forums on its Web site. Individuals can post short comments about any P&G product or join longer discussions where they interact with other visitors about specific P&G products. Having more focused discussion areas may help to create a community of interaction where individuals feel comfortable sharing their opinions: P&G, for example, recognizes that the people who want to talk about Oil of Olay may not be the same people as those who wish to discuss Charmin Toilet Paper.

At the Kraft Foods Web site a discussion forum titled "Wisdom of Moms" allows visitors to share thoughts and ideas on more general topics. For example, one general topic recently featured asked visitors to share tips and ideas for starting summer off on the right foot. These postings tended to feature novel ways to use different Kraft products that were timesaving and transportable for summer fun. These ideas could then be used in promotions, recipes, and other communications. At both sites, visitors are told that any comments become the property of the Web site sponsor (i.e., either P&G or Kraft). Links to the company's privacy policies are also clearly marked. Thus, visitors can understand their legal rights regarding the discussion forum participation.[5]

Role of the Moderator.   It is possible that the account planner will serve as the moderator for the open-ended group, or another designated individual could take on the moderator function. Regardless, the role of the moderator should be clearly defined. The moderator should encourage and respond to postings so visitors can see that their comments are appreciated and valued. Beyond that, you must decide to what degree the moderator should monitor the posting on the discussion forum. Given that participants can post a message to the discussion board at any time, it is possible that discussions not germane to the client will begin and flourish. Generally, these are termed "off-topic" or "OT" discussions and evolve as participants become comfortable with the discussion forum and with each other. They signify that an online community is forming. However, they do take up bandwidth and may draw attention away from the topics that are important to you.

Establishing Policy. The anonymous nature of open-ended groups may allow individuals to participate who are not interested in the discussion but merely wish to stir up conflicts, evoke anger, and disrupt the harmony of the discussion forum. Online, these individuals are known as "trolls." Trolls may post messages that call participants and/or their postings stupid, they may post derogatory or obscene messages, and in general they may try to create a negative environment on the discussion forum. Trolls usually go away if ignored. However, given the potential for such postings on your discussion forum, it is best to develop a policy upfront about deleting inappropriate messages and let posters know about the policy.

It is probably better to err on the side of having more off-topic information than getting a reputation for the discussion forum being so heavily moderated that a variety of opinions are not getting posted. You should, however, clearly indicate on the discussion forum (perhaps in a discussion forum procedures topic) the types of messages that will not be tolerated (obscenities, hate messages, etc.). The moderator can then delete these posts. Also be sure to put a message on the site that anything posted to the site belongs to the company and will be used for research purposes. Such a message could read:

> This is a Moderated Area. All messages posted to this board become the property of [client's name] and will be used only for research purposes. Use of the board is a privilege, not a right. Excessive foul language and/or vengeful or hateful posts will not be tolerated.

You should also have a policy on client participation on the discussion forum. Clients should be involved, yet they should be discouraged from posting or getting into arguments/discussions with participants in the discussion forum. Communication with the moderator regarding the postings is important and can help steer the forum discussion to areas that are of interest to all parties.

Software. As with the closed-ended focus groups, a variety of software options are available, ranging from creating a discussion forum at a free site like http://www.ezboard.com/ and linking to the discussion forum from your Web site, to creating a proprietary message discussion forum at your client's site. Free sites often function by providing advertising messages adjacent to the discussion forum, which may be somewhat distracting.[6] Again, we recommend that you discuss the options with your IT people to determine the best option for meeting your client's needs.

Recruitment. Recruiting participants for an open-ended group can be accomplished in the same ways as for the closed-ended focus group (i.e., you could run banner ads directing individuals to the site, or you could purchase e-mail lists and send individuals e-mails inviting them to visit the site). However, you can also simply create links to the discussion forum on the client's Web site and recruit persons to visit the discussion forum from visitors to the Web site. Of course, this would limit the participants to people who are already interested for some reason in the client's products or services. By waiting for persons to visit the site, it may take longer to gather the initial set of responses. However, it is possible that individuals will continue to visit the discussion forum to view what others have said about the topic, and interactions among participants (and the moderator) can begin and flourish.

Screening.   In general, any and all individuals are encouraged to post at an online discussion forum; in this way participants create their own community and will freely interact with and respond to the moderator. You should decide whether participants should be able to post without registering or if you would prefer people to register before posting. Registration can involve asking for a simple screen name and e-mail address. Either way, participants are allowed to be anonymous, which may make their responses richer and more real. However, accepting anonymous responses does not mean giving up moderator control. It is possible to delete off-topic posts as well as to block individuals from posting on the discussion forum, especially if individuals have to register to post. However, be cautious about the frequency of deleting posts or blocking individuals because excessive moderator control may minimize visitor participation.

The Actual Session.   The nature of an open-ended session suggests that the discussion forum will be in operation for at least a week or two, at minimum, and can possibly become a staple on the Web site. The account planner should decide how often new topics will be posted. For example, you could post a topic of the day or topic of the week so visitors will know that there will always be something new to talk about at the discussion forum. After a question or topic has run its course (say, after a month or 6 weeks) the discussion can be closed so the discussion forum will not become too cluttered. Understand your target audience, and be sure you write to the reading level of the people who will be visiting and participating at your site.

The moderator should feel free to respond to other people's posts, not only to encourage participation ("What an interesting idea! What does everyone else think about that?"), but also to probe for additional information ("Can you explain a bit more about that idea?"). Questions or discussion topics can be posted quickly, easily, and inexpensively, and frequent updates to questions will encourage participants to continually check back to the site. The moderator should plan to check the discussion forum at least twice a day.

In some ways, the moderator has more control over the open-ended experience than can be provided during a closed-ended session because the moderator can provide specific questions for discussion, along with more in-depth background material on issues related to the topic. Visitors can access additional information via links, and participants can develop a relatively deep level of understanding of a topic. In addition, the moderator can have more control because it is very difficult for an individual to dominate a message forum. It is fairly simple to moderate the discussion forum because conversations do not require immediate intervention on the part of a moderator.

There are obvious trade-offs, however, in that there is less control over issues such as timing and quality of postings because it is impossible to know when people will be visiting and responding to the discussion forum. Even with a twice-a-day check of the discussion forum, there is a risk that an off-topic discussion will start and take over the discussion forum before the moderator has a chance to pull the discussion back to the original topic. It is also difficult to show stimuli (such as advertisements) without having individuals leave the discussion forum. This is problematic, because it is possible that participants will view the stimuli and then neglect to return to the discussion forum to post their thoughts.

As with closed-ended focus groups, you will lose visual cues from the individuals who are responding to the discussion forum. You cannot read their facial expressions or sense when they are being sincere or sarcastic. Thus, you may misinterpret some statements, and others participating on the discussion forum may also misinterpret them. The risk is that a misinterpretation could escalate into a conflict that would not be noticed by the moderator until after some amount of time has passed. This may result in participants' having negative feelings about the discussion forum and perhaps wishing not to return.

After the Session.   As previously mentioned, a cut-off time for each topic should be established (e.g., every 4 to 6 weeks), but the planner should analyze data as postings occur and not wait until the cut-off time to begin analysis. However, flexibility for the cut-off date is essential: If a topic is "hot," you might think about letting it run for a few more days or a week. Similarly, if no one is responding to a topic, you may wish to delete it from the discussion forum in order to avoid a cluttered appearance. The account planner/moderator should determine the frequency of reviewing and updating the clients on the discussion forum postings. Again, this may change based on the frequency of postings and how involved the discussion becomes.

If participants register to enter into the discussion forum site, be sure to ask them if they would like to receive e-mails from you in the future (also called "opting in"). Send e-mails periodically (say, once a month or so) to those who opt in, reminding them to check the discussion forum to continue to participate in the dialogue. Do not send them such messages too often, though, or you may be considered a spammer.

As with a closed-ended focus group, you will have the transcript immediately available for evaluation. It can be evaluated similarly to an offline group's transcript.

Depth Interviewing

The final type of online qualitative research involves conducting depth interviews. These can be done either via e-mail or in a chat room. E-mail is preferred for several reasons. People around the world have access to e-mail; a recent survey suggested that 50% of Internet users use e-mail on a daily basis (Rainie & Packel, 2001). Even individuals who are hesitant to use chat rooms or to download software from the Web are comfortable with e-mail. E-mail has become a fairly standard way of communicating for many people, and it may even seem more traditional and comfortable for them than participating in a chat room or an online focus group.

There are many advantages to online interviewing. First, individuals can respond in their own time without the pressure of having to be at a certain place for a certain amount of time. This may allow for a broader range of people to agree to participate in a depth interview. For example, busy executives may be more willing to commit to an e-mail interview than other types of interviews. E-mail interviews are excellent for interviewing shy people. E-mail often allows for direct contact with individuals, thus avoiding secretaries, PR departments, and the like. In addition, conflicting time zones and schedules are avoided; it is possible to interview individuals around the world, day and night. E-mail allows the account planner to contact people all over the world without having the expense of flying to their hometowns to interview them. E-mail can be used not only to conduct the interview, but also to schedule the interview itself and to double-check statements and probe for additional comments (Young, Persichitte, & Tharp, 1998).

E-mail interviews are good for receiving highly technical information, as the interviewee is creating the information him- or herself and thus generating the transcript. Any miscommunication about technical aspects of a topic can be avoided, and questions about technical terminology can be returned to the interviewee for clarification. Giving someone the luxury of composing an answer (as opposed to quickly giving an off-the-cuff answer) may take some of the spontaneity away from the response, but it also allows the interviewee to craft a thoughtful response to your question, regardless of the complexity.

The lack of the physical presence of an interviewer may also be a benefit in some situations. For example, asking questions about appearances and physical characteristics may be easier in an e-mail situation, where the participant does not have to look at the interviewer or feel that the interviewer is looking for a certain response. In this way biases may be minimized.

There are a few drawbacks to e-mail interviews. E-mail interviews may not allow the interviewer to get a good sense of the person being interviewed due to a lack of physical interaction. E-mail itself does not allow for a free flow of information back and forth, give and take, or serendipitous digressions. Occasionally, e-mail responses sound canned or contrived. Online interviews would not be appropriate in situations where understanding an individual's emotions would be important; discussing a tragedy, say, or a deeply personal issue would not work well in an e-mail environment. Topics that are more impersonal may work better for online interviews.

PREPLANNING

As with an in-person interview, the majority of the preplanning time will be devoted to developing the questions to be asked. It is recommended that no more than 10 questions be included in the e-mail interview message; if necessary, you can send follow-up e-mails to probe or to gather additional information from the individuals. The following are some tips about e-mail interview questions:

- Questions should, of course, be open-ended: Be sure questions can't be answered with a simple yes or no. The better the opportunity for people to say what is on their minds and to talk about themselves, the better the responses will be.
- Questions should be clear, uncomplicated, and as short as possible. Start with a straightforward, easy question, and then probe attitudes and feelings.
- Number each question and leave space for a reply.
- Be sure that your final question allows interviewees to provide any additional comments on the topic that they wish.

Keep in mind that many different types of e-mail readers exist. Many Web-based e-mail programs and programs such as Microsoft Outlook have the capacity to display not only text, but also images. However, many users still use text-only based e-mail programs (such as Pine) or may adjust their browsers to exclude images in order to speed download times. Therefore, exposing participants to anything other than text-based questions or information in the interview is best accomplished through links to other sites online where participants can view the image.

RECRUITMENT

Individuals are recruited for an online interview in the same way as an offline interview; the big difference is the mode in which the interview will take place. Therefore, if you are recruiting individuals via telephone, make sure that they have e-mail access and are comfortable with answering questions via e-mail. If you are using e-mail to recruit individuals, never send an unsolicited e-mail with a series of questions to a potential participant. The recipient is likely to consider this presumptuous at the least and an invasion of his or her privacy at the worst.

In the e-mail solicitation, describe the types of questions that will be asked and indicate the approximate number of questions that will be included. Indicate that you may have follow-up questions that would be provided to the participant after the initial response. Give the individual some idea of your timetable, such as when the questions will be sent, when a reply is needed, and when any follow-up questions will be provided. You may also wish to find out whether the participants use e-mail in only one location and whether they will have consistent access to their e-mail during the interview period (Young et al., 1998).

Regardless of the mode used, you should use this recruitment time to develop a rapport with the participants. By putting them at ease with this new type of interview process, you will model response patterns that they will ideally emulate during the actual interview.

THE ACTUAL INTERVIEW

You are about to press the "send mail" key to send your interview questionnaire out to your participants. However, before you send the message, you should be sure that, in addition to the questions, some specific information is included in the e-mail.

You should provide instructions on how the questions should be physically entered into the return e-mail—either by typing in an answer underneath each question or by labeling each answer with the appropriate question number. Also, the participants may be more comfortable sending the message back via postal mail or fax. Provide all possible addresses and telephone numbers for such responses.

In addition, you should be sure to remind your participants of the date you need their answers returned to you, and to thank them for taking the time to answer your questions. Also, advise them that you will likely be following up with them within a set period of time (say, within 24 hours of receiving the e-mail) to ask for clarification or more information on specific topics. In that way, the participants will be expecting your follow-up and, it is hoped, will respond promptly to any additional questions you have.

IF YOU DON'T RECEIVE A REPLY

Like a teenager waiting by the telephone to be invited to the prom, you will probably be checking your e-mail constantly to see if people are responding to your questions. It can be disheartening if you don't receive replies right away. Remember, your participants are living busy lives, and though your research may be a priority for you, it may not be for them.

If you haven't received a return e-mail with the questions answered by your specified date, send a short e-mail message to the laggards reminding them of the interview and requesting that they respond to the interview at their earliest convenience. Offer to answer any questions or concerns they have either via e-mail or via telephone. Also, offer to send another copy of the questions to them, in case they cannot easily access the e-mail in their e-mail inbox.

WHEN THE E-MAIL ARRIVES

As soon as you receive responses, be sure to let each participant know the e-mail has been received and to reinforce that you may be sending out follow-up questions. Be timely with the sending of the follow-up questions and include specific text from answers that you wish participants to comment further on in case they didn't save a copy of their original responses. Try to limit the follow-up questions to five or fewer; with more, participants may feel they are being asked to participate in yet another interview that is beyond their original commitment, and they may not be as forthcoming with their answers.

If you are planning to compensate participants, let them know how and when that payment will be made in the e-mail that you send confirming the receipt of the interview.

DATA ANALYSIS

One benefit of the e-mail interview is that the transcript is immediately available for analysis. Analysis should proceed as responses are returned to you and should be conducted using the same analysis techniques described earlier in this book.

As with all qualitative interviews, you should allow the participant to see the transcript and make any revisions. This transcript can be sent via a file attachment to e-mail. Provide a specific time by which you would like the participants to return their comments regarding the interview to you.

Informing Participants

The Internet offers a new realm of possibilities for qualitative interviews. However, just because the mode is different doesn't mean that the research standard of informed consent and participation can be ignored. You should always make sure participants understand that they are participating in a research project and be upfront with them about how the information will be used. Be respectful of information that they do not wish to provide. Be prompt and courteous in your online communication, and think of e-mail "netiquette" when you interact online: Be careful to spell correctly, don't type in all capital letters (people will think you're yelling), and answer all questions about this new technique as completely and quickly as you can.

Becoming an Internet-savvy researcher requires a time commitment from you because the technology is rapidly changing and keeping on top of developments takes some effort. Nevertheless, we believe the effort is well worth it, because advertising agencies are constantly trying to keep up with new technology and to understand the best way to harness the power of the Internet for their clients. If you can be at the forefront of this development, you will position yourself as a highly valuable member of the account team.

Summary

The Internet provides new ways for account planners to connect with and learn about all types of consumers. Conducting research online can be accomplished through closed-ended focus groups (via a chat room), open-ended focus groups (via a discussion forum), and long interviews (via e-mail). Although online consumer research should never fully replace talking with and observing consumers in their natural setting, there are several situations where the Internet can allow you to contact hard-to-reach individuals and engage them in the research process. Certain topics, especially ones involving technology, also are appropriate for online research.

If you decide to conduct qualitative research on the Internet, you should be comfortable with online communication and recognize that traditional methods cannot simply be replicated for the online environment. Communication must be somewhat more explicit to make up for the lack of visual and audio cues that accompany in-person research. As with all research, upfront preparation is key to make sure that online research is successful.

In the next chapter, we shift our focus to an examination of the creative brief. The creative brief is probably the most important document that you as the account planner will develop. You've spent weeks observing, talking to, and understanding consumers and their motivations; you now have the opportunity to make these consumers come alive for the creative team. The creative brief is the way that happens.

Key Terms

Chat room: Internet site where "real-time" interaction among multiple individuals occurs

Closed-ended focus group: Small group of people brought together in chat-room format at a specific time to answer questions posed by a moderator

Discussion forum: Internet site where individuals can post messages regarding specified topics

List broker: Entity selling individual e-mail addresses

Off topic: Posts on a discussion forum that are not germane to the specified topic of discussion

Open-ended focus group: Online discussion forum where an unlimited number of participants can respond to questions posed by a moderator

Opt-in: Process by which individuals agree to receive unsolicited e-mail

Spam: Unsolicited commercial e-mail (UCE); e-mail not requested by an individual

Troll: Individual attempting to disrupt discussions at open-ended focus groups

Exercises

1. Set up a discussion forum connected to your company, department, or class's Web page. Be sure to check with higher-ups for permission, and find an IT person to help you out if necessary. Focus the discussion on topics that can provide information to your administration about key issues among your colleagues and peers. You may want to ask questions like, "What do you like best about this department?" or, "What would you like to change about our building?" Monitor this forum for several weeks and provide a summary of your findings.

2. Recruit several friends to participate in an e-mail interview about their favorite restaurants in your community. Prepare a series of questions, conduct the interviews via e-mail, and identify patterns in the data. You may want to ask questions like, "Tell me why this is your favorite restaurant. What makes this restaurant different from other restaurants? How do you feel when you're at this restaurant?" Share your findings with others who do the exercise to see if there are any commonalities in the data.

Related Reading

Jones, S. (1999). *Doing Internet research: Critical issues and methods for examining the Net.* Thousand Oaks, CA: Sage.

Mann, C., & Stewart, F. (2000). *Internet communication and qualitative research: A handbook for researching online.* Thousand Oaks, CA: Sage.

Turkle, S. (1995). *Life on the screen: Identity in the age of the Internet.* London: Simon & Schuster.

Notes

1. For information on recruiting via banner ads on DoubleClick, visit www.doubleclick.net/us/.

2. Many companies sell targeted e-mail address lists. A list of such companies can be found at http://list-advertising.com/opt-in/.

3. A brief review of ethical research practices can be found at http://trochim.human.cornell.edu/kb/ethics.htm.

4. For simple instructions on creating and accessing a free chat room via Yahoo, visit http://spectrum.troyst.edu/~sstokes/help/y_chat.htm.

5. If your clients do not have a privacy policy, encourage them to visit the Direct Marketing Association's Web site (http://www.the-dma.org/) for information on what should be included in a corporate online privacy policy.

6. For a description of a free bulletin board/discussion forum service, visit http://www.net-gate.net/html/bbs_how_to.html. A comprehensive list of bulletin board/discussion forum services is available at http://wsabstract.com/howto/forum2.shtml.

7

Briefing the Team

Writing and Presenting the Creative Brief

Nothing strikes fear into the hearts of copywriters and art directors as much as the sight of an account planner standing at their office door with a ream of research results in her arms. It's not that the creative team doesn't want to learn about the consumer; in fact, art directors and copywriters appreciate this information because creatives aren't necessarily representative of the people to whom the advertising will be targeted. However, the way you inform the team about the consumer is what this chapter is about. A major part of the account planner's job is to determine the best way to present consumer information to the creative team. This involves several skills, including the ability to distill the information into a manageable and inspirational form, as well as the ability to communicate the information to the creative team in a way that best stimulates creative development.

The focus of this chapter is the *creative brief*. Note we use the term creative *brief*, not creative strategy or creative platform, despite the fact that you also come across the latter two in the advertising world. We think of the creative brief in a very literal way. The word brief means concise, free of superfluous detail. That's what your creative brief should be: the crux of all your investigations into products and consumers with all the superfluous stuff taken out. Jon Steel (1998) described the creative brief as the bridge between strategic thinking and advertising. The creative brief sets the boundaries within which the art director, copywriter, creative director, and others involved in message creation can do what they do the best: create effective and memorable advertising. Similarly, Lisa

Fortini-Campbell (1992) has described the creative brief as the document that "introduces the creative department to the person they'll be talking to." In that way, the creative brief is "an advertisement to influence the creative team" (Steel, 1998, p. 149).

Because the creative brief begins a dialogue at the start of the creative process, the process of sharing the creative brief with the creative team is as important as the content of the creative brief itself. We begin this chapter with a discussion of the relationship between the account planner and the creative team. Then, we discuss why agencies develop creative briefs, describe what elements account planners commonly use in creative briefs, and provide tips on the language that is appropriate for the creative brief. This chapter also discusses how the creative brief is shared with the team—a meeting known as the creative briefing—and provides guidelines for this important meeting.

Account Planners and the Creative Team

The original manifesto developed by the British Account Planning Group stated that

> in the advertising world no one has a monopoly over wisdom or ideas; an agency consists of a group of people with different skills, abilities, experience and person- alities trying very hard to get the best possible advertising for their clients. (British Account Planning Group, 2001)

A good relationship between the account planner and the creative team (i.e., the copywriter and art director, and possibly the creative director) is based on trust and cooperation. The creative team must trust that the information brought by the account planner is accurate and focused. Few things can ruin this relation- ship more than research that is perceived to be irrelevant or unnecessary. In talk- ing with various creatives from different agencies across the United States as we prepared this book, we found one story in particular that exemplifies this point.

We asked various creatives about their relationship with planners and how they wanted research insights to be presented. One Chicago creative, whom we will refer to as RK, responded,

> It's [meaning research] all useless! I never will forget one time when this young kid stood up in front of us to say that all the research lead to one conclusion, "the number one reason people buy ketchup is the taste." For crying out loud! You just spent $40,000 to tell me that? Give me something useful or shut up.

You wouldn't want to be on the receiving end of that tirade, would you? Encounters like this with research led RK not to want to have anything to do with planners or research. He commented, "Creatives get paid to reach people. I know how to do that without all this research bunk."

The good news is that most of the creatives we spoke with who worked in planning agencies saw value in planning, and they reported good relationships with their planners. We strongly feel that for planning to be optimally effective the account planner, creatives, and other members of the strategy team must be willing to work synergistically to execute the strategy. To develop a good relationship with the creative team, an account planner must establish a dialogue with the team members about the research problem at hand. To develop this relationship we recommend the following:

- Recognize that every creative team is different. Get to know each of the copywriters and art directors you're working with and understand how the team works, particularly how they like to get information. Watch them interact with other creative teams and with account managers to better understand their communication style better. Find out what motivates them. Take them to lunch when you aren't working under a deadline, and learn who they are as indivi-duals, just like you would with any consumer!
- Seek the copywriter's and art director's advice early in the process, particularly regarding strategic issues. Ask them about their experiences with other clients. What did they perceive as problems and benefits of using research in the past? This type of discussion fosters an early sense of trust.
- Share the passion that the copywriter and art director have for advertising. Advertising is their art. Recognize that no idea is a bad idea, and work with the team to create polished diamonds out of their rough ideas.
- Inspire, don't instruct. Remember, you're all part of the same team, working toward the same goal. You're not the boss of the creative team, you are a member of the team.

What Is the Role of the Creative Brief?

The creative brief is a communications tool. As noted earlier, the account planner uses the creative brief to begin a dialogue with the creative team regarding the advertising that is to be developed. The term brief recognizes that the relationship between account planners and the creative team is an equal one, and one group (i.e., the account planner) is not giving orders or instructions to another group (i.e., the creative team). Therefore, the development of the creative brief and its presentation to the creative team should not reflect boss to subordinate communication. Instead, think of the creative brief as a peer-to-peer communication that is persuasive and enlightening but not dictatorial.

Before we delve into writing a creative brief, it's important to note that different agencies approach the creative brief in different ways. We are working on the assumption that the actual creative brief will be in written format and presented to the creative team. In some agencies, however, the creative brief is delivered in memo form to the creative team and a briefing is not held. Conversely, other agencies do not allow written creative briefs, and the creative briefing is the only tool by which information is shared. The norm, however, appears to be that agencies use both a written creative brief and a creative briefing. In many agencies, the individual responsible for the creative brief is the account planner, although it may be the account executive or a team of the planner and account executive. From this point on, we assume that the account planner is the author of the creative brief.

The Account Planner and the Creative Brief

You may ask, "If a brief is supposed to begin a dialogue with the creative team, then why do I need to put it in writing?" That's a good question, and one that begs us to examine the purposes of a creative brief. The creative brief begins the dialogue with the creative team by setting the boundaries within which the advertising will be developed. It serves several other purposes, too. Creative briefs are documents of how advertising messages are developed. Both agency and client personnel can review several years of creative briefs that can illustrate the development of any particular brand. The creative brief is also a point of agreement among everyone involved on the advertising at both the agency and the client. Clients will be asked to approve the creative brief, thereby indicating their agreement to the strategic direction of the creative brief. This can be especially beneficial if client personnel change during the course of the campaign development. The signed-off creative brief is in essence a contract that will provide clients an indication of what the advertising will communicate, and it may mitigate potential conflicts during a personnel change. Having a written document is also seen as beneficial to many creative teams, in that they can continuously refer to the creative brief to keep them on track as they develop the advertising. Finally, the creative brief allows the agency and client account teams to develop a somewhat objective evaluation of the advertising, because the communication achieved by the advertising can be compared to the communication goals set out in the creative brief.

We mentioned earlier in this chapter that we spoke with various creatives from planning agencies in preparation for this book. The vast majority (except for a few like our dear friend RK) felt that good creative briefs were extremely helpful to them. Usually, these creatives would begin their answer to our question about how they would prefer research insights to be presented by saying something to the effect of, "Don't bring me reams of paper." Then they would talk about the value of a good planner's ability to synthesize the research and help them begin the creative strategy process by bringing the marketing situation to life. Various academic studies support what we found in our interviews with creatives. For example, Arthur Kover and Stephen Goldberg (1995) interviewed creative teams in both Detroit and New York and found that, when creating advertising, copywriters and art directors often engage in one-on-one conversations with an internalized targeted consumer. As part of that process they accept and welcome "the creative brief and other consumer-based sources of information to help them flesh out the target person" (Kover & Goldberg, 1995, p. 600). This finding was confirmed in a survey of creative officers in many of the top U.S. agencies (Reid, King, & DeLorme, 1998).

Because the creative brief is the starting point for the development of the creative execution, it's likely that there will be revisions to the creative brief as the account planner acquires new knowledge about consumers or about the environment under which the creative brief is being developed. In this sense, the brief should be viewed as a dynamic and evolving document. For example, during the creative briefing, the creative team may have additional insights about the brand that they learned from working on other accounts. These would be incorporated into a revision of the creative brief. If a competitive brand begins a campaign that uses elements similar to your brand's creative brief, then the account planner may reevaluate and rewrite the creative brief given the changes in the advertising environment.

Though the brief may evolve during the development of the advertising, it is important for one individual to be the main author and the "keeper" of the creative brief. One reason this is important is that the creative brief must commit to a point of view, and having a single person in charge of the creative brief best ensures this commitment. The author must also be able to defend the creative brief and its point of view to others. A single author will best understand the complete thought process that went in to writing the creative brief and will be best able to both defend and "sell" it.

Writing the actual creative brief is a process that takes time; it is best not to try to hammer it out whenever you have a free half hour. The process of writing a creative brief takes a great deal of analysis and reflection by the account planner. The account planner should begin with a clear idea about what both the client and the agency want the advertising to achieve. This advertising goal may be in terms of sales, impressions, attitudes, or awareness, or some combination of these, and relate specifically to the goals set out in the client's marketing plan. The account planner must also think about the information that must be included in the message and the information that must be avoided. Most important, the account planner must review the accumulated data about the brand, the target audience, and the market in order to determine which of the key insights derived from the research is most likely to resonate with the target audience. The key insight that is distilled from all the information received through the research process becomes the essence of the account planner's point of view.

Obviously, this key insight is the focal point of the creative brief (Fortini-Campbell, 1992). The account planner will need to have an internal dialogue with him- or herself regarding the various insights derived from the research, and the benefits and detriments of using each of them as the key insight to the brand. The planner may also seek opinions from others involved in the process, such as the creative team and the account people, as well as from other planners who may have additional ideas about the advertising challenge facing the brand. Brainstorming and discussing the various pros and cons of different strategic alternatives is a good way to distill the many ideas into the single most important thought that will motivate consumers to take the action that will meet the communication goals. Once the account planner intrinsically believes that the key insight has been found, and has the research to back up the relevance of the key insight, he or she can turn to the actual crafting of the creative brief.

The Basics of the Creative Brief

Many agencies have their own formats and/or formulas for what goes into a creative brief. Most creative briefs encompass the following items.

OBJECTIVE OR STATEMENT OF PURPOSE

In this first section, account planners address questions such as, Why are we advertising? What is the problem that advertising can solve? How will the client benefit? How will consumers benefit? The objective will be closely related to the marketing goals established by the client in the marketing plan (Roman & Maas, 1992). If there are several levels of marketing goals, you will need to prioritize them carefully and assess which are best addressed through advertising. John Furgurson (2000) suggests that you address no more than two marketing objectives in the brief; otherwise, the message will be diluted, and you may set yourself up for failure.

TARGET AUDIENCE

The creative brief should focus on the consumer and present the advertising challenge from his or her perspective. This section describes the consumer from numerous perspectives: demographically, psychographically, and in terms of product/service usage and behavior. Jon Steel says that the brief should contain a portrait of a consumer that is descriptive and emotional (Steel, 1998). Look for truths that bind different consumers together, aspects of their lives that are meaningful (Furgurson, 2000). The target audience description should give insight into how consumers think and feel; Fortini-Campbell (1992) describes this section as the way to put the consumer at the table with all other members of the advertising team.

COMPETITION

Both short-term and long-term competitors should be identified. For a spaghetti sauce product, for example, short-term competition might be all other jarred sauces, longer-term competition might include canned tomatoes, tomato paste, packaged sauce mixes, and other bases that a cook could use to create a sauce to his or her taste.

CHOSEN COMMUNICATION

This is sometimes termed the "key insight," "single most important thought," or "promise"; it is what you hope consumers will take away from the advertising message. The insight will pull together all the research and show how it fits into the bigger context of the advertising message. The techniques described earlier in this book should help you to discover the key consumer insights that will motivate consumers to purchase your brand. The consumer insight should be linked with a brand insight for maximum impact (Fortini-Campbell, 1992). Also included in this section is the support, or reasons why the target will believe the message focus. Support points can include both product attributes and consumer attitudes.

MANDATORY INCLUSIONS/EXCLUSIONS

The creative team needs to know if there is any information that must or must not be included in the advertisement. This is often included in the advertising itself for legal reasons. For example, advertising for many types of bank products must by law include specific financial disclosure information. Occasionally, the creative team may need to be reminded of industry advertising guidelines for specific product categories. For example, the beer beverage industry has a guideline that adults not be shown actually drinking beer in commercials.